The Sayings of Sri Ramakrishna

SWAMI ABHEDANANDA

COSIMO CLASSICS

NEW YORK

God is nearer to you than anything else,
yet because of egoism you cannot see Him.

—Sri Ramakrishna

OM NAMO BHAGAVATE RAMAKRISHNAYA.

SALUTATIONS TO BLESSED RAMAKRISHNA!

PREFACE.

THIS volume will supply the demand of those whose interest in the unsectarian teachings of Bhagavân Sri Râmakrishna Paramahamsa has been aroused by the Blessed Swâmi Vivekânanda's celebrated work entitled "My Master." It contains almost all of the valuable Sayings of this great Hindu Saint of the nineteenth century, translated from Bengâli in which the Bhagavân originally spoke.

An attempt has also been made for the first time to classify and arrange in logical sequence the Sayings which were published in the "Brahmavâdin," "The Awakened India," as well as in "Râmakrishna, His Life and Sayings," by Professor Max Muller, all having been carefully compared with the original and revised.

May these Sayings enlighten the minds and broaden the spiritual ideals of the Western nations in the same manner as they have done in the East is the earnest prayer of Sri Râmakrishna's disciple,

SWÂMI ABHEDÂNANDA.

v

"Will you be able to practise as much as I tell you? If you live up to one-sixteenth part of what I say unto you, you will surely reach the goal."

GOD.

1. You see many stars at night in the Existence of God. sky but find them not when the sun rises; can you say that there are no stars in the heaven of day? So, O man! because you behold not God in the days of your ignorance, say not that there is no God.

2. Many are the names of God and infinite the forms that lead us to know Him. In whatsoever name or form you desire to call Him, in that very form and name you will see Him.

3. As one and the same material, water, Oneness of God. is called by different names by different peoples, one calling it water, another *eau*, a third *aqua*, and another *pani*, so the one Sat-chit-ânanda, the everlasting-Intelligent-Bliss, is invoked by some as God, by some as Allah, by some as Jehovah, by some as Hari, and by others as Brahman.

4. In a potter's shop there are vessels of different shapes and forms,—pots, jars, dishes, plates, etc., but all are made of one clay. So God is one, but is worshipped in different ages and climes under different names and aspects.

God's aspects many. 5. *Q.* If in all the religious systems of the world there reigns the same God, then why does the same God appear different when viewed in different light by different religions?

A. God is one, but many are His aspects. As one master of the house appears in various aspects, being father to one, brother to another and husband to a third, so one God is described and called in various ways according to the particular aspect in which He appears to His particular worshipper.

6. As one can ascend to the top of a house by means of a ladder or a bamboo or a staircase or a rope, so divers are the ways and means to approach God, and every religion in the world shows one of these ways.

Sri Ramakrishna.

7. Different creeds are but different All creeds
paths to reach the Almighty. Various **paths to**
and different are the ways that lead to the **God.**
temple of Mother Kâli at Kâlighat (near
Calcutta). Similarly, various are the
ways that lead to the house of the Lord.
Every religion is nothing but one of such
paths that lead to God.

8. As with one gold various ornaments
are made, having different forms and
names, so one and the same God is
worshipped in different countries and
ages under different forms and names.
Though He may be worshipped in accord-
ance with different conceptions and
modes,—some loving to call Him father,
others mother, some calling Him friend,
others calling Him the beloved, some praying to Him as the inmost treasure of
their hearts, calling Him the sweet little
child, yet it is one and the same God that
is being worshipped in all these relations
and modes.

9. As the young wife in a family shows
her love and respect to her father-in-law,
mother-in-law, and every other member

of the family, and at the same time loves her husband more than these; similarly, being firm in thy devotion to the Deity of thy own choice (Ishta-Devata), do not despise other Deities, but honor them all.

10. Bow down and worship where others kneel, for where so many have been paying the tribute of adoration the kind Lord must manifest Himself, for He is all mercy.

11. As the same sugar is made into various figures of birds and beasts, so the one Sweet Mother Divine is worshipped in various climes and ages under various names and forms.

God with form and formless. 12. Two persons were hotly disputing as to the color of a chameleon. One said, "The chameleon on that palm tree is of a beautiful red color." The other, contradicting him, said, "You are mistaken, the chameleon is not red but blue." Not being able to settle the matter by arguments, both went to the person who always lived under that tree and had watched the chameleon in all its phases of color. One of them said, "Sir, is not the chameleon on that tree of a red color?" The person replied, "Yes, sir." The other disputant said, "What do you say? How is it? It is not red, it is blue." That person again humbly replied, "Yes, sir." The person knew that the chameleon is an animal that constantly changes color; thus it was that he said "yes" to both of these conflicting statements.

The Sat-chit-ânanda likewise has many forms. The devotee who has seen God in one aspect only, knows Him in that aspect alone. But he who has seen Him in manifold aspects is alone in a position to say, "All these forms are of one God and God is multiform." He is formless and with form, and many are His forms which no one knows.

13. Fire itself has no definite shape, but in glowing embers it assumes certain forms. The formless fire is then endowed with forms. Similarly the formless God sometimes invests Himself with definite forms.

14. So long as the sound of a bell is audible, it exists in the region of form;

but when it is no longer heard, it has become formless. Similarly God is both with form and formless.

Nature of Brahman. 15. *Q.* What is the nature of Brahman (God)?

A. The Brahman is without attributes, unchangeable, immovable, and firm like Mount Meru.

16. His name is Intelligence (Chinmaya). His abode is Intelligence, and He, the Lord, is All-intelligence.

17. The Lord can pass an elephant through the eye of a needle. He can do whatever He likes.

18. The sun is many times larger than the earth but distance makes it look like a very small disk; so the Lord is infinitely great, but being too far away from Him we fail to comprehend His real greatness.

19. God is absolute eternal Brahman as well as the Father of the Universe. The indivisible Brahman, pure Existence, Intelligence and Bliss, is like a vast, shore-

Sri Ramakrishna.

less ocean without bounds and limits in which I only struggle and sink, but when I approach the always sportive Personal Deity, *Hari*, I get peace like the sinking man who finds the shore.

20. As water when congealed becomes ice, so the visible form of the Almighty is the condensed manifestation of the All-pervading formless Brahman. It may be called, in fact, Sat-chit-ânanda solidified. As ice is part and parcel of water, remains in water and afterwards melts in it; so the Personal God is part and parcel of the Impersonal. He rises from the Impersonal, remains there, and ultimately merges into it and disappears.

Personal and Impersonal God.

21. God is formless and God is with form too, and He is that which transcends both form and formlessness. He alone can say what else He is.

22. At a certain stage of his path of devotion the devotee finds satisfaction in God with form; at another stage, in God without form.

23. The God with form is visible, nay, we can touch Him face to face, as with one's dearest friend.

24. As the same fish is dressed into soup, curry, or cutlet, and each has his own choice dish of it, so the Lord of the Universe, though One, manifests Himself differently according to the different likings of His worshippers, and each one of these has his own view of God which he values the most. To some He is a kind master or a loving father, a sweet smiling mother or a devoted friend, and to others a faithful husband or a dutiful and obliging son.

Mâyâ and Brahman. 25. *Q.* What is the relation between Mâyâ and Brahman?

A. Mâyâ may be compared to a snake that is active and moving, while Brahman is like the snake absolutely still. Mâyâ is the name of the manifested powers of the Absolute and Immovable Reality which is called Brahman.

26. Falling in the meshes of phenomena, the ever-Blissful Brahman appears to weep and wail.

16

Sri Ramakrishna.

27. In the course of his instructions to his disciple, the Guru raised two fingers by which he meant the duality of "Brahman and Mâyâ," then lowering one finger, he taught him that when Mâyâ vanishes, nothing of the universe remains but the one Absolute Brahman.

28. Who could have realized the Absolute Brahman if there were no Mâyâ and her manifestations?

29. *Q*. Can Brahman be described? *A*. It cannot be explained by words. As a man called upon to give an idea of the ocean to a person who has never seen it, can only say, "It is a vast sheet of water, a big expanse of water, it is water—water all round"; so one who has realized Brahman can only say, "Brahman, Brahman is everywhere." **Brahman cannot be described by words.**

30. He who tries to give an idea of God by mere book learning, is like the man who tries to give an idea of Kasi (Benares) by means of a map or picture.

31. The Vedas, Tantras, and the Puranas and all the sacred scriptures of the

world have become as if defiled (as food thrown out of the mouth becomes polluted), because they have been constantly repeated by and have come out of human mouths. But the Brahman or the Absolute has never been defiled, for no one as yet has been able to express It by human speech.

God with and without attributes. 32. At one time I am clothed, at another naked, so Brahman is at one time with attributes and at another without.

33. God is like unto a hill of sugar. A small ant carries away from it a small grain of sugar, a bigger one takes from it a considerably larger grain. But the hill remains as large as before. So are the devotees of God. They become ecstatic with even a grain of one Divine attribute. No one can contain within him all His attributes.

God and Soul. 34. *Q.* God is infinite, the creature or *Jiva* a finite being. How then can the finite grasp the Infinite?

A. It is like a figure of salt trying to fathom the depths of the ocean. In doing so the salt doll is dissolved into the sea and lost. Similarly the *Jiva*, in trying to measure God, loses his individual egoism and becomes one with Him.

35. As a piece of lead thrown into a basin of mercury soon becomes dissolved, so the individual soul melts away, losing its limitations, when it falls into the ocean of Brahman.

36. What is the relation between the individual ego (Jivâtman) and the Supreme Spirit (Paramâtman)?

A. As when a plank of wood is stretched across a current of water, the water seems to be divided into two, so the Indivisible appears divided into two by the limitations (Upâdhi) of Mâyâ. In fact they are one and the same.

Relation between individual ego and Supreme Spirit.

37. The soul enchained is "man" (Jiva) and free from chains is "God" (Shiva).

38. As the water and its bubble are one: the bubble has its birth in the water, floats on the water, and ultimately is resolved into water; so the individual ego

The Sayings of

(Jivâtman) and the Supreme Spirit (Paramâtman) are one and the same. The
difference is in degree, the one is finite and
small, the other is infinite; the one is de-
pendent, the other independent.

39. So long as one is not blessed with
the vision Divine, so long as the base metal
is not turned into gold by touching the
philosopher's stone, there will be the delusion of "I am the doer," and so long
must there necessarily remain the idea
of the distinction between "I have done
this good work, and I have done that bad
work." This idea of duality or distinction is the Mâyâ which is responsible for
the continuance of the world current.
By taking refuge in *Vidyâmâyâ* (the Mâyâ
having preponderance of *satva*), which
follows the adoption of the right path,
one can reach Him. He alone crosses the
ocean of Mâyâ who comes face to face
with God, who realizes Him. He is truly
free, living even in this body, who knows
that God is the doer and he is the non-doer.

40. What is the nature of the union of
the Jivâtman (human soul) and the Para-

Sri Ramakrishna.

mâtman (Supreme Spirit)? It is like the union of the hour and the minute hands at twelve o'clock.

41. God is in all men but all men are not in God: that is the reason why they suffer.

42. God is related to man as magnet is to iron. Why does not then God attract man? As iron thick imbedded in mud is not moved by the attraction of the magnet, so the soul thick imbedded in Mâyâ feels not the attraction of the Lord. But as when the mud is washed away with water the iron is free to move, so when the soul by constant tears of prayer and repentance washes away the mud of Mâyâ that makes it cleave to the earth, it is soon attracted by the Lord.

God related to man.

43. The magnetic needle always points towards the North, and hence it is that the sailing vessel does not lose her course. So long as the heart of man is directed towards God, he cannot be lost in the ocean of worldliness.

44. The loadstone rock hidden under the sea attracts the ship sailing over it, draws out all its iron nails, separates plank from plank, and sinks the vessel into the sea. Even so, when the magnet of God-consciousness attracts the human soul, it destroys in a moment man's sense of earthly personality and selfishness and plunges the soul into the ocean of God's Infinite Love.

45. As a lamp does not burn without oil, so man cannot live without God.

Yearning for God. 46. Verily, verily, I say unto you that he who yearns for God finds Him.

47. He finds God quickest whose yearning and concentration are greatest.

48. Like unto a miser that longeth after gold, let thy heart pant after Him.

49. Men weep rivers of tears because a son is not born to them, others wear away their hearts with sorrow because they cannot get riches. But how many are there who weep and sorrow because they have

Sri Ramakrishna.

not seen God? He finds who seeks Him; he who with intense longing weeps for God has found God.

50. As the child beseeches its mother with importunities for toys and pice, weeping and teasing her, so he who knows God to be his nearest and dearest, his own, and who like an innocent child weeps inwardly with earnestness to see Him, is rewarded at last with the vision of Divine Beauty. God can no longer remain hidden from such an earnest and importunate seeker after Him.

51. Verily, verily, I say unto thee, he who longs for Him, finds Him. Go and verify this in thine own life; try for three consecutive days with genuine earnestness and thou art sure to succeed.

52. "I must attain perfection in this life, yea, in three days I must find God; nay, with a single utterance of His name I will draw Him unto me." With such a violent love the Lord is attracted soon. The lukewarm lovers take ages to go to Him, if at all.

The Sayings of

53. What offering is required to attain to God? To find God, thou must offer Him thy body, mind, and riches.

Search after God.

54. A thief enters a dark room and feels the various articles therein. He lays his hand upon a table, perhaps, and saying "Not this," passes on; he comes in contact with some other article—a chair, perhaps—and again saying "Not this," he continues his search, till leaving article after article, he finally lays his hand on the box containing the treasure; then he exclaims "It is here," and there his search ends. Such is indeed the search after Brahman.

55. Adopt adequate means for the end you seek to attain. You cannot get butter by crying yourself hoarse saying "There is butter in the milk." If you wish to make butter, turn the milk into its curds and churn it well, and then you will get butter. So if you seek to see God, practise spiritual Sâdhan (devotional exercises) and then you will see God. What is the good of merely crying "O God, O God !"?

24

Sri Ramakrishna.

56. Be diluted in the Supreme Spirit.

57. Meditate on God either in an unknown corner, or in the solitude of forests, or within your own mind.

58. Should we pray aloud to God?
A. Pray unto Him in any way you like. He is sure to hear you, for He can hear even the footfall of an ant.

59. So long as a man calls aloud "Allah Ho! Allah Ho!" ("O God! O God!") be sure that he has not yet found his Allah (God), for he who has found Him becomes quiet and full of peace.

60. Q. Where is the Lord and how is He to be found?
A. There is pearl in the deep sea, but one must hazard all perils to get it. So is the Lord in this world.

61. If a single dive into the sea does not bring to you the pearl, do not conclude that the sea is without pearls. Dive again and again and you are sure to be rewarded in the end. So if your first

attempt to see God proves fruitless, do not lose heart. Persevere in the attempt and you are sure to obtain Divine grace at last.

62. *Q.* How may we find our God?

A. The angler, anxious to hook a big and beautiful Rohitta fish, waits calmly for hours together, having thrown the bait and the hook into the water, watching patiently until the bait is caught by the fish. Similarly, the devotee who patiently goes on with his devotions is sure at last to find his God.

How to see God. 63. *Q.* If God is omnipresent, why do we not see Him?

A. Standing by the bank of a pool thickly overspread with scum and weeds, you will say that there is no water in it. If you desire to see the water, remove the scum from the surface of the pond. With eyes covered with the film of Mâyâ you complain that you cannot see God. If you wish to see Him, remove the film of Mâyâ from off your eyes.

64. As the cloud covers the sun, so Mâyâ conceals the Deity. When the

26

Sri Ramakrishna.

cloud moves away, the sun is seen; so when Mâyâ is removed, God becomes visible.

65. As fishes playing in a pond covered over with reeds and scum cannot be seen from outside, so God plays in the heart of a man invisibly, being screened by Mâyâ from human view.

66. God cannot be seen so long as there is the slightest taint of desire; therefore have thy small desires satisfied, and renounce the big desires by right reasoning and discrimination.

67. None can enter the kingdom of Heaven if there be the least trace of desire in him, just as a thread can never enter the eye of a needle if there be any slight detached fibre at its end.

68. As to approach a monarch one must ingratiate oneself with the officials who keep the gate and surround the throne, so to reach the Almighty one must practise many devotions, as well as serve many devotees and keep the company of the wise.

69. The intoxication of hemp is not to be had by repeating the word "hemp." Get the hemp, rub it with water into a solution and drink it, and you will get intoxicated. What is the use of loudly crying "O God, O God!"? Regularly practise devotion and verily you shall see God.

Name of the Lord. 70. The truly devotional and spiritual practice suited to this Kali-Yuga (Iron Age) is the constant repetition of the name of the Lord of Love.

71. If thou wishest to see God, have firm faith in the efficacy of repeating the name of *Hari* (Lord) and try to discriminate between the real and unreal.

72. Consciously or unconsciously, in whatever way one falls into the trough of nectar, one becomes immortal. Similarly, whosoever utters the name of the Deity voluntarily or involuntarily finds immortality in the end.

73. It is the nature of the lamp to give light. With its help some may cook food,

Sri Ramakrishna.

some may forge a deed, and the third may read the Word of God. So with the help of the Lord's name some try to attain salvation, others try to serve their evil purposes and so on. His holy name, however, remains unaffected.

74. Knowingly or unknowingly, consciously or unconsciously, in whatever state we utter God's name, we acquire the merit of such an utterance. As a man who voluntarily goes to a river and bathes therein gets the benefit of the bath, so does he too who has been pushed into the water by another, or who, when sleeping soundly, has water thrown upon him.

75. The truly wise man is he who has seen the Lord. He becomes like a child. He who has seen the Lord. The child, no doubt, seems to have an Ahamkâra, an egoism, of its own; but that egoism is a mere appearance, it is not selfish egotism. The self of a child is nothing like the self of a grown-up man.

76. The Self (Aham) of the child is again like the face reflected in the mirror. The face in the mirror looks exactly like

the real face; only it does nobody any
harm.

77. *Q.* Will all men see God?

A. No man will remain in total fast;
some get their food at 9 A.M., others at
noon, others at 2 P.M. and others in the
evening at sunset. Similarly, at some
time or other, in this life or after many
lives, all will see God.

**God re-
vealeth
Himself.** 78. The watchman can see with a dark
lantern (bull's-eye) every one on whom
he throws its rays, but no one can see him
so long as he does not turn the light upon
himself. So does God see every one, but
no one seeth Him until the Lord revealeth
Himself to him in His mercy.

79. *Q.* Why can we not see the Divine
Mother?

A. She is like a high-born Hindoo lady
transacting all her business from behind
the screen, seeing all but seen by none.
Her devout sons only see Her, by going
near Her behind the screen of Mâyâ.

80. A mother has several children. To
one she has given a bit of coral, to another

Sri Ramakrishna.

a doll, and to a third some sweets, and thus, absorbed in their playthings, they all forget their mother; and she in the meanwhile goes on with her household work. But among them the child who throws away his playthings and cries after the mother, "Mamma, dear Mamma"— she runs quickly to him, takes him in her arms and caresses him. So, O man! you have forgotten your Divine Mother, absorbed in the vanities of the world; but when you throw them off crying after Her, She will come at once and take you up in Her arms.

81. Oh heart! Call out truly to thy Almighty Mother, and thou shalt see how she will come quickly running to thee. When one calls out to God with all one's heart and soul, He can no longer remain unmoved.

82. The landlord may be very rich, but when a poor ryot brings a humble present to him with a loving heart, he accepts it with the greatest pleasure. So the Almighty God, though so great and powerful, accepts the humblest offerings of a

God accepts humblest offering.

31

sincere heart with the greatest pleasure and kindness.

83. Howsoever far may be the fishes in a pond, when sweet, attractive and savory bait is thrown into the water, they soon hasten to that point from all quarters. Similarly the Lord approaches quickly the holy devotee whose heart is full of devotion and faith.

God's advent in human heart. 84. *Q.* What are the indications of God's advent in the human heart?

A. As the dawn heralds the rising sun, so unselfishness, purity, and righteousness precede the advent of the Lord.

85. As a king, before going to the house of a servant to receive hospitality there, sends from his stores the necessary seats, ornaments, articles of food, etc., to the servant so that this latter may properly receive and honor his master; so before the Lord cometh, He sendeth Love, Reverence, and Faith into the yearning heart of the devotee.

God-vision. 86. *Q.* In what condition of the mind does God-vision take place?

Sri Ramakrishna.

A. God is seen when the mind is tranquil. When the mental sea is agitated by the wind of desires, it cannot reflect God and then God-vision is impossible.

87. So long as the heavenly expanse of the heart is troubled and disturbed by the gusts of desire, there is little chance of our beholding therein the brightness of God. The beatific vision occurs only in the heart which is calm and rapt in divine communion.

88. God is attained when man reaches maturity in either of these three states: (1) "All this am I," (2) "All this art Thou," (3) "Thou the master and I the servant."

89. As the woman who is fully devoted to her husband is called Sati (chaste) and obtains the love of her lord, so the man who is fully devoted to his special Deity obtains God.

90. The steel sword is turned into a golden sword by the touch of the philosopher's stone, and though it retains its

The Sayings of

He who
hath be-
held God
doeth no
evil. former form, it becomes incapable of injuring any one like the steel sword. Similarly the outward form of the man who has touched the feet of the Almighty is not changed, but he no longer doeth any evil.

91. The Lord he has seen and he is now a changed being.

92. So long as a man is far away from the market, he hears only a loud and indistinct buzzing sound like Ho!! Ho!! But when he enters the market place, he no longer hears the uproar, but perceives distinctly that some one is bargaining for potato, another for brinjal and so on. As long as man is far away from God, so long is he in the midst of the buzzing noise and confusion of reasoning, argument and discussion; but when he approaches God, then cease all reasoning, argument and discussion, and he understands the mysteries of God with clear and vivid perception.

93. In the play of hide and seek, if the player succeeds in touching the non-player

Sri Ramakrishna.

who is called grand-dame (Boori), he is no longer liable to be made a thief by the seeker. Similarly by once seeing the Almighty, a man is no longer bound down by the fetters of the world. Just as the person touching the *Boori* is free to go about wherever he chooses without being pursued and made a thief of, so also in this world's playground there is no fear for him who has touched the feet of the Almighty. He attains freedom from all worldly cares and anxieties and nothing can ever bind him again.

94. Milk mixes readily with water when brought into contact with it. Convert it into butter, however, and it no longer mixes with the water but floats upon it. So when the soul once attains the state of God, it may live in constant and hourly contact with innumerable unregenerate souls but will not at all be affected by their evil association.

95. Iron, if once converted into gold by the touch of the philosopher's stone, may be kept under the ground or thrown into a rubbish heap; it always remains

35

The Sayings of

gold and will never return to its former condition. Similar is the state of him who has at heart touched even once the feet of the Almighty. Whether he dwells in the bustle of the world or in the solitude of the forest, nothing will ever contaminate him.

He who knows God indifferent to worldly pleasures. 96. He who has once tasted the refined and crystalline sugar-candy, finds no pleasure in raw treacle; he who has slept in a palace will not find pleasure in lying down in a dirty hovel. So the soul that has once tasted the sweetness of the Divine Bliss finds no delight in the ignoble pleasures of the world.

97. She who has a king for her lover will not accept the homage of a street beggar. So the soul that has once found favor in the sight of the Lord does not want the paltry things of this world.

98. A recently married young woman remains deeply absorbed in the performance of domestic duties so long as no child is born to her. But no sooner a son is born to her than she begins to neglect

Sri Ramakrishna.

household details and does not find much pleasure in them. Instead thereof, she fondles the new-born baby all the live-long day and kisses it with intense joy. Thus man in his state of ignorance is ever busy in the performance of all sorts of works, but as soon as he sees in his heart the Almighty, he finds no pleasure in them. On the contrary, his happiness consists now only in serving God and doing His works. He no longer finds happiness in any other occupation and cannot withdraw himself from the ecstasy of that Holy Communion.

99. Knowledge and Love of God are ultimately one and the same. There is no difference between pure knowledge and pure love. Knowledge and Love of God.

100. The Knowledge of God (Jnâna) may be likened to a man, while the Love of God (Bhakti) is like a woman. Knowledge has entry up to the outer rooms of God, but no one can enter the inner apartments (the zenâna) of God save Love, which has access into the mysteries of the Almighty.

The Sayings of

101. Shiva and Sakti (The Absolute and power) are both necessary for creation. With dry clay no potter can make a vessel, water is necessary. So Shiva alone cannot create without Sakti or force.

Worship of Images.

102. As a toy fruit or a toy elephant reminds one of the real fruit and the living animal, so do the images worshipped remind one of God who is formless and eternal.

103. Bhagavân Sri Râmakrishna, addressing Keshab Chandra Sen, who was a great iconoclast in his day, said: "Why do these images raise the idea of mud and clay, stone and straw in your mind? Why can you not realize the presence of the eternal, blissful, all-conscious Mother even in these forms? Know these images to be concretised forms of the eternal and formless essence of all sentiency.

104. If a man thinks of the images of gods and goddesses as symbols of the Divine, he reaches Divinity. But if he considers them as mere idols made of stone, straw and clay, to him the worship of those images produceth no good.

38

Sri Ramakrishna.

105. The master said, "Everything that God in exists is God." The pupil understood it every-literally, but not in the right spirit. While thing. he was passing through the street he met an elephant. The driver (Mâhout) shouted aloud from his high place, "Move away!" "Move away!" The pupil argued in his mind, "Why should I move away? I am God, so is the elephant God; what fear has God from Himself?" Thinking thus, he did not move. At last the elephant took him up in his trunk and dashed him aside. He was hurt severely, and going back to his master, he related the whole adventure. The master said: "All right. You are God, the elephant is God also, but God in the shape of the elephant-driver was warning you from above. Why did you not pay heed to his warnings?"

106. We cannot say that God is gracious because He feeds us, for every father is bound to supply his children with food; but when He keeps us from going astray and holds us back from temptations, then He is truly gracious.

107. It is the nature of the child to soil itself with dirt and mud, but the mother

The Sayings of Sri Ramakrishna.

Man's Re- does not allow it to remain dirty always;
demption. she washes it from time to time. So it
is the nature of man to commit sin, but
sure as it is that he commits sin, it is
doubly sure that the Lord creates means
for his redemption.

108. The darkness of centuries is dis-
persed at once as soon as a light is brought
into the room. The accumulated sins of
innumerable births vanish before a single
gracious glance of the Almighty.

God with- 109. Pointing to the heart, the Bhaga-
in Man. vân used to say: "He who has it here,
has it also there (pointing to the external
world). He who does not find God
within himself will never find Him outside
himself. But he who sees Him in the
temple of his soul, sees Him also in the
temple of the universe."

" Mother! destroy in me all idea that I am great, and that I am a Bråhmin, and that they are low and pariahs, for who are they but Thou in so many forms?"

SAVIOURS, SAGES, AND SPIRITUAL TEACHERS.

110. The Avatâra or Saviour is the messenger of God. He is like the viceroy of a mighty monarch. As when there is some disturbance in a far-off province, the king sends his viceroy to quell it, so whenever there is a decline of religion in any part of the world, God sends His Avatâra there.

Saviour Messenger of God.

111. It is one and the same Avatâra that, having plunged into the ocean of life, rises up in one place and is known as Krishna, and diving down again rises in another place and is known as Christ.

112. The Avatâras (like Râma, Krishna, Buddha, Christ) stand in relation to the Absolute Brahman as the waves of the ocean are to the ocean.

43

The Sayings of

113. When Bhagavân Srî Râmachándra came to this world, seven sages only could recognize Him to be the God incarnate. So when God descends into this world, few only can recognize His Divine nature.

114. None knoweth the immensity of the sacrifice which the Godhead maketh when It becomes incarnate in a human form.

Redeeming power of Saviours. 115. In some seasons water can be obtained from the great depths of the wells only, and with great difficulty, but when the country is flooded in the rainy season, water is obtained with ease everywhere. So, ordinarily, God is reached by saints with great pains through prayers and penances, but when the flood of Incarnation descends, Divine manifestation is seen anywhere and everywhere, and by his grace everybody is saved.

116. As a large and powerful steamer moves swiftly over the waters, towing along flats and barges in its wake; so when a Saviour descends, He easily carries thousands across the ocean of Mâyâ.

44

Sri Ramakrishna.

117. The locomotive engine reaches the destination itself and also draws and takes with it a long train of loaded wagons. So likewise act the Saviours: they carry multitudes of men heavily laden with sin into the presence of the Almighty.

118. On the tree of absolute Existence- **Saviours** Knowledge-Bliss (Sat-chit-ananda) there **many.** hang innumerable Râmas, Krishnas, Buddhas, Christs, etc., out of which one or two come down to this world now and then and produce mighty changes and revolutions.

119. Think not that Sitâ, Râma, Srî, Krishna, Râdhâ, Arjuna, etc., were not historical personages, but mere allegories, or that the Scriptures have an inner and esoteric meaning only. Nay, they were beings of flesh and blood just as you are, but because they were Divinities, their lives can be interpreted both historically and spiritually.

120. There is a fabled species of birds called "Homâ," which live so high up in the heavens, and so dearly love those

regions, that they never condescend to come down to the earth. Even their eggs, which when laid in the sky begin to fall down to the earth attracted by gravity, are said to get hatched in the middle of their downward course and give birth to the young ones. The fledgelings at once find out that they are falling down and immediately change their course and begin to fly upwards towards their home, drawn thither by instinct. Men such as Suka Deva, Nârada, Jesus, Sankarâchârya, and others, are like those birds, who even in their boyhood give up all attachments to the things of this world and betake themselves to the highest regions of true Knowledge and Divine Light.

121. As the elephant has two sets of teeth, the external tusks and the inner grinders, so the God-Men like Srî Krishna and others act and live like common men to the view of all, while their souls rest far beyond the pale of Karma.

122. *Q*. When the Jews nailed the body of Jesus on the Cross, how was it that Jesus, in spite of so much pain and suffering, prayed that they should be forgiven?

Sri Ramakrishna.

A. When an ordinary cocoanut is pierced through, the nail enters the kernel of the nut too; but in the case of the dry nut the kernel becomes separate from the shell and when the shell is pierced, the kernel is not touched. Jesus was like the dry nut, i.e., His inner soul was separate from His physical shell, consequently the sufferings of the body did not affect Him. Though the nails were driven through and through, He could pray with peace and tranquillity for the good of His enemies.

123. There are two sorts of men. The Guru said to one of his disciples, "What I impart to thee, my dear, is invaluable, keep it to thyself"; and the disciple kept it to himself. But when the Guru imparted that knowledge to another of his disciples, the latter, knowing its inestimable worth and not liking to enjoy it alone, stood upon a high place and began to declare the good tidings to all the people. The Avatâras are of the latter class, while the Siddhas (perfect ones) are of the former. *Avatâras and Siddhas.*

124. When the flood comes, it inundates rivers and streams and makes one

watery surface of all adjacent lands; but
the rain water flows away of itself through
fixed channels. When a Saviour incarnates, all are saved through His grace.
The Siddhas (perfect ones) only save
themselves with much pain and penance.

125. A Siddha-purusha (perfect man)
is like an archeologist who removes the
dust and lays open an old well which has
been covered up during ages of disuse by
rank growth. The Avatâra, on the other
hand, is like an engineer who sinks a new
well in a place where there was no water
before. Great men can give salvation
to those only who have the waters of piety
hidden in themselves, but the Saviour
saves him too whose heart is devoid of all
love and dry as a desert.

126. When a mighty raft of wood floats
down a stream, it carries on it hundreds
and does not sink. A reed, floating
down, may sink with the weight of even a
crow. So when a Saviour incarnates,
innumerable are the men who find salvation by taking refuge under Him. The
Siddha only saves himself with much
toil and trouble.

Sri Ramakrishna.

127. What is the state which a Siddha attains? (A perfect man and well-cooked food are both called Siddha. There is a pun here on the word Siddha.)

As potato or brinjal when Siddha, i.e., when boiled properly, becomes soft and pulpy; so man when he becomes Siddha, i.e. reaches perfection, is seen to be all humility and tenderness.

128. Five are the kinds of Siddhas found in this world: **Kinds of Siddhas.**

(1) The Swapna-Siddhas are those who attain perfection by means of dream-inspiration.

(2) The Mantra-Siddhas are those who attain perfection by means of a sacred mantra or formula.

(3) The Hathat-Siddhas are those who attain perfection suddenly, like a poor man who suddenly becomes rich by finding a hidden treasure or by marrying into a rich family; so many sinners become pure all of a sudden and enter the kingdom of heaven.

(4) The Kripa-Siddhas are those who attain perfection through the tangible grace of the Almighty, as a poor man is

made wealthy by the kindness of the king.

(5) The Nitya-Siddhas are those who are ever perfect. As a gourd or a pumpkin creeper brings forth fruit first and then its flowers, so the ever-perfect soul is already born a Siddha and all his seeming exertions after perfection are merely for the sake of setting examples to humanity.

129. Is it possible for a human soul to obtain the condition of absolute union with God when he is able to say "Sohum," "He is I?" If so, how? This is just like the case of an old servant of a house who in the course of time comes to be counted as a member of the family. When the master of the house becomes very much pleased with the servant's work, he one day takes it into his fancy and gives him his own seat of honor, saying to all the members of the household: "Henceforth there shall be no difference between him and me. He and I are one. Obey his commands as ye do mine, and he who fails to do so, disobeys my orders and will be punished for it." Even though the servant may hesitate through modesty to

Sri Ramakrishna.

occupy the seat, yet the master compels him to take the seat of honor. Similar to this is the condition of souls who reach the state of "Sohum," "He is I." When they serve the Lord for a long time, He graciously endows some of them with all His glory and attributes and raises them to His own seat of Universal Sovereignty.

130. The Divine sages form, as it were, the inner circle of God's nearest relatives· They are like friends, companions, kinsmen of God. Ordinary beings form the outer circle or are the creatures of God. **Divine Sages.**

131. The sage alone can recognize a sage. He who deals in cotton-twists can alone tell of what number and quality a particular twist is.

132. A sage was lying in a deep state of Samâdhi by a roadside; a thief passing by saw him and thought within himself: "This fellow lying here is a thief. He has been breaking into some house by night and now sleeps exhausted. The police will very soon be here to catch him. So let me escape in time." Thus think-

ing, he ran away. Soon after a drunkard came upon the sage and said: "Hallo! thou hast fallen into the ditch by taking a peg too much. I am steadier than thou and am not going to tumble." Last of all there came a sage, and understanding that a great sage was in Samâdhi, he sat down, touched him reverently, and began to rub gently his holy feet.

Perfect Man unpolluted by world. 133. A perfect man is like a lotus leaf in the water or like a mud-fish in the marsh. Neither of these is polluted by the element in which it lives.

134. As an aquatic bird, such as a pelican, dives into water, but the water does not wet its plumage, so the emancipated soul lives in the world, but the world does not affect him.

135. The swan can separate the pure milk from the water with which it has been mixed; it drinks only the milk, leaving the water untouched. Other birds cannot do so. So God is intimately mixed up with Mâyâ; ordinary men cannot see Him separately from Mâyâ. Only the

Sri Ramakrishna.

Paramahamsa (the Great Soul: here is a pun on the word *hamsa*, which means both soul and swan) rejects Mâyâ and takes up God only.

136. Some Great Souls who have reached the seventh or the highest plane of Samâdhi and have thus become merged in God-consciousness, are pleased to come down from that spiritual height for the good of mankind. They keep the ego of knowledge (the *aham* of *Vidyâ*) or, in other words, the higher Self. But this ego is a mere appearance; it is like a line drawn across a sheet of water. *(margin note: Great souls retain only semblance of egoism.)*

137. After the attainment of Samâdhi some have the ego—the ego of the servant, the ego of the devotee. Sankarâchârya kept the ego of Vidya (knowledge) for the teaching of others.

138. The Master's talk with a disciple:
Master: Have I any *abhiman* (egoism)?
Disciple: Yes, a little and that little has been kept with a view to the following objects: first, the preservation of the body; second, the culture of Bhakti or

53

devotion to God; third, the desire to mix in the company of Bhaktas (devotees); fourth, the desire to give instruction to others. At the same time it must be said that you have kept it only after a good deal of *prayer*. My idea is that the natural state of your soul is capable of being described only by the word *Samâdhi*. Hence I say that the *abhiman* or egoism that you possess is the result of *prayer*.

Master: Yes, but *it is not I that have kept it* (this self) *but it is my Divine Mother.* It lies with my Divine Mother to grant the prayer.

139. Hanumana was blessed with the vision of God both Sâkâra and Nirâkâra (with form and without form). But he retained the ego of a servant of God. Such was also the case with Narada, Sanaka, Sananda, and Sanatkumara.

(Here the question was asked if Narada and others were Bhaktas only and not Jnânis too. The Bhagavân said:)

Narada and others had attained the highest knowledge (Brahmajnâna). But still they went on like the murmuring waters of the rivulet talking and singing.

54

Sri Ramakrishna.

This shows that they too kept the ego of knowledge—a slight trace of individuality to mark their separate existence from the Deity,—for the purpose of teaching others the saving truths of Religion.

140. As a rope that is burnt retains its form intact, but, being all ash, nothing can be bound with it, so the man who is emancipated retains merely the form of his egoism, but no idea of self (Ahamkâra).

141. When the head of a goat is severed from its body, the trunk moves about for some time, still showing the signs of life. Similarly, though the *Ahamkâra* (egoism) is beheaded in the perfect man, yet sufficient of its vitality is left to make such a man carry on the functions of physical life; but that much is not sufficient to bind him again to the world.

142. Ornaments cannot be made of pure gold. Some alloy must be mixed with it. A man totally devoid of Mâyâ will not survive more than twenty-one days. So long as the man has a body, he must have some Mâyâ, however small it may be, to carry on the functions of the body.

The Sayings of

143. The wind carries the odor of the sandalwood as well as that of ordure, but does not mix with either. The emancipated soul in the same way lives in the world but does not mix with it.

Preaching of Perfect Ones. 144. When a fire burns the moths come, one knows not whence, and they fall into it and die. The fire is not seen to invite the moth to its fate. Similar to this is the preaching of the perfect ones. They do not go about calling others, but hundreds come to them of their own accord, no one knows whence, to get instruction from them.

145. Hast thou got, O Preacher, the badge of authority? As the humblest servant of the king authorized by him is heard with respect and awe, and can quell the riot by showing his badge; so must thou, O Preacher, obtain first the order and inspiration from God. So long as thou hast not this badge of Divine inspiration thou mayest preach all thy life, but only in vain.

146. What is true preaching like? Instead of preaching to others, if one wor-

Sri Ramakrishna.

ships God all that time, that is enough preaching. He who strives to make himself free is the real preacher. Hundreds come from all sides, no one knows whence, to him who is free, and are taught by him. When a rosebud blooms, the bees come from all sides uninvited and unasked.

147. Throw an unbaked cake of flour into hot *ghee* (butter), it will make a sort of boiling noise. But the more it is fried, the less becomes the noise; and when it is fully fried, the bubbling ceases altogether. So long as a man has little knowledge, he goes about lecturing and preaching, but when the perfection of knowledge is obtained, man ceases to make vain displays.

148. *Q.* What do you think of the man who is a good orator and preacher, but whose spirituality is undeveloped?

A. He is like a person who squanders another's property kept in trust with him. He can easily advise others, for it costs him nothing, as the ideas he expresses are not his own but borrowed.

Spiritually undeveloped as preachers.

57

149. *Q.* What is your opinion about the methods employed by present-day religious preachers?

A. It is like inviting a hundred persons to a dinner when the food supply is sufficient for only one. It is pretending to be a great religious teacher with a small stock of spiritual experience.

150. As many have merely heard of snow but not seen it, so many are the religious preachers who have read only in books about the attributes of God, but have not realized them in their lives. And as many have seen but not tasted it, so many are the religious teachers who have got only a glimpse of Divine glory, but have not understood its real essence. He only who has tasted the snow can say what it is like. Similarly, he alone can describe the attributes of God who has associated with Him in His different aspects, now as a servant of God, then as a friend of God, then as a lover of God, or as being absorbed in Him.

151. The light of the gas-lamp illumines various localities with varying

Sri Ramakrishna.

intensity, but the life of the light, namely, God, the
the gas, comes from one common reser- one
voir. So the religious teachers of all source of
all teach-
climes and ages are but so many lamp- ing.
posts through which is emitted the light
of the spirit flowing constantly from one
Almighty Source.

152. As the rain water, falling upon the
roof of a house, flows down to the ground
through pipes having their mouth-pieces
shaped like the head of a tiger or a bull
and appears to come out of tigers' mouths,
but in reality it descends from the sky;
even so the eternal truths that come out
of the mouths of godly men are not uttered
by those men themselves, but in reality
descend from the kingdom of heaven.

153. What is the reason that a prophet Prophet
is not honored by his own kinsmen? The without
honor at
kinsmen of a juggler do not crowd round home.
him to see his performances while stran-
gers stand agape at his wonderful tricks.

154. The seeds of *Vajrabantul* do not
fall to the bottom of the tree. They are
carried by the wind far off and take root
there. So the spirit of a prophet mani-

fests itself at a distance and he is appreciated there.

155. There is always a shadow under the lamp while its light illumines the surrounding objects. So the men in the immediate proximity of a prophet do not understand him. Those who live far off are charmed by his spirit and extraordinary power.

156. The Divine power must be understood to be in greater quantity in those who are honored, respected and obeyed by a large following than in those who have no such influence.

Good and holy Sâdhus alone reflect Divine Light.

157. The sunlight is one and the same wherever it falls, but only bright surfaces like water, mirrors and polished metals can reflect it fully. So is the Light Divine. It falls equally and impartially on all hearts, but only the pure and clean hearts of the good and holy Sâdhus (holy ones) can fully reflect it.

158. He alone is the real man who is illumined by the light of true knowledge. Others are men but in name.

Sri Ramakrishna.

159. That knowledge which purifies the intellect is the true knowledge, everything else is non-knowledge.

160. The companionship of the holy and wise is one of the main elements of spiritual progress. **Society of the pious.**

161. The society of pious men is like the water in which rice is washed. The rice-water dissipates intoxication. So doth the society of the pious relieve worldly men, intoxicated with the wine of desire, from their intoxication.

162. How should one pass one's life? As the fire on the hearth is stirred from time to time with a poker to make it burn brightly and prevent it from going out, so the mind should be invigorated occasionally by the society of the pious.

163. The agent of a rich Zemindâr, when he goes into the mofussil or interior, tyrannises in various ways over the tenants. But when he comes back to the headquarters under the eyes of his master, he changes his ways, becomes very pious,

treats the tenants kindly, investigates
all their grievances fully, and tries to mete
out impartial justice to all. The tyran-
nical agent becomes good through the fear
of the landlord and by the effect of his
society. Similarly doth the society of the
pious make even the wicked righteous,
awakening awe and reverence within
them.

164. The moist wood placed upon a
fire soon becomes dry and ultimately
begins to burn. Similarly the society
of the pious drives away the moisture of
greed and lust from the hearts of worldly
men and women, and then the fire of
Viveka (Discrimination) burns in them.

165. As the blacksmith keeps alive the
fire of his furnace by the occasional blowing of his bellows, so the mind should be
kept burning by the society of the pious.

Guru or
Spiritual
Teacher.
166. If thou art in right good earnest
to be good and perfect, God will send the
proper Master (*Sad-Guru*) to thee. Earnestness is the only thing necessary.

Sri Ramakrishna.

167. So long as the mind is unsteady and fickle it availeth nothing, even though a man has got a good Guru and the company of holy men.

168. The fabled pearl-oyster leaves its bed at the bottom of the sea and comes up to the surface to catch the rainwater when the star Svâti is in the ascendant. It floats about on the surface of the sea with its shell wide open until it succeeds in catching a drop of the marvellous Svâti-rain. Then it dives down to its sea bed and there rests until it has succeeded in fashioning a beautiful pearl out of that raindrop. Similarly, there are some true and eager aspirants who travel from place to place in search of that watchword from a godly and perfect preceptor (*Sad-Guru*) which will open for them the gate of eternal bliss; and if in their diligent search one is fortunate enough to meet such a Guru and get from him the much-longed-for *logos* which is sure to break down all fetters, he at once retires from society and enters into the deep recess of his own heart and rests there till he has succeeded in gaining eternal peace.

169. The Man-Guru whispers the sacred
formula into the ear: the Divine Guru
breathes the spirit into the soul.

"The Man-Guru *mantra* to ears doth impart,
The God-Guru seals it on tablets of heart."

170. The Guru is a mediator. He
brings man and God together.

Necessity of one Guru. 171. *Q.* What is the necessity of calling
a particular man Guru instead of every
one who teaches us something?

A. As when going to a strange country
one must abide by the directions of the
guide who knows the way, while acting
upon the advice of many may lead to confusion; so in trying to reach God, one must
follow implicitly the advice of one single
Guru who knows the way to God.

172. Whoever can call on the Almighty with sincerity and intense earnestness of soul needs no Guru. But such
a deep yearning of the soul is very rare,
hence the necessity of the Guru. The
Guru is only one, but Upa-Gurus may be
many. He is an Upa-Guru from whom
anything whatsoever is learned. The

Sri Ramakrishna.

great Avâdhuta had twenty-four such Upa-Gurus.

173. He who thinks his spiritual guide (Guru) to be a mere man cannot derive any benefit from him.

174. The disciple should never criticise his Guru. He must implicitly obey what- **Disciple must not criticise Guru.** ever the Guru says. Says a Bengâli couplet:

> "Though my Guru may visit tavern and still,
> My Guru is holy Rai Nityananda still."

"Though my Guru may visit the unholy rendezvous of drunkenness and sinners, still to me he is my own pure and faultless Guru."

175. Take the pearl and throw the oyster shell away. Follow the *mantra* (advice) given thee by thy Guru and throw out of consideration the human frailties of thy teacher.

176. Listen not if any one criticises and censures thy Guru. Leave his presence at once.

The Sayings of

177. He who considers his Guru to be
human, what fruit can he get from his
prayers and devotions? We should not
consider our Gurus to be mere men.
Before the disciple sees the Deity, he
sees the Guru in the first vision of divine
illumination, and it is the Guru who afterwards shows the Deity, being mysteriously
transformed into the form of the Deity.
Then the disciple sees the Guru and the
Deity to be one and the same. Whatever
boon the disciple asks, the deified Guru
even gives him that, yea, the Guru even
takes him to the highest bliss, Nirvâna.
Or the man may choose to remain in a
state of duality, maintaining the relation
of a worshipper and the worshipped.
Whatever he asks, his Guru vouchsafes
him that.

Guru facilitates spiritual progress. 178. In a play of dice called *Ashta-kashte* the pieces must pass through all the squares of the checker-board before they reach the central square of rest and non-return. But so long as a pawn does not reach that square, it is liable to return again and again to its starting-point and commence its weary journey many times

66

Sri Ramakrishna.

over. If however two pawns happen to
start their journey in unison and move
jointly from square to square, they cannot be forced back by any winner. Similarly in the world, those who start in their
career of devotional practices, first uniting
themselves with their Guru and Ishta
(chosen Ideal), need fear no reverses and
difficulties and their progress will be
smooth, unimpeded, and without any
retrogression.

179. As in mid-ocean a bird, which has
found its perch upon the topmast of a
ship, getting tired of its position, flies
away to discover a new place of rest for
itself, and alas! without finding any,
returns at last to its old roost upon the
masthead, weary and exhausted; so when
an ordinary aspirant, being disgusted with
the monotony of the task and the disci-
pline imposed upon him by his well-
wishing and thoroughly experienced Guru
(spiritual guide), loses all hopes and,
having no confidence in him, launches
forth into the broad world ever in search
of a new guide, he is sure at last to return
to his original master after a fruitless

search, which has, however, increased the reverence of the repentant aspirant for his own Guru.

180. "Gurus (teachers) can be had by hundreds of thousands, but a good *chela* is very rare," is an ancient saying. It means that many are the persons who can give good advice, but they who follow it are few.

181. Who can be another's Guru? God alone is the Guru and Master of the universe.

Sann-yâsins. 182. *Q.* Who is the fit candidate for the holy order of Sannyâsins?

A. He who gives up the world altogether without taking thought for the morrow as to what he shall eat or wherewithal he shall be clothed, is a true Sannyâsin. He is like a man who climbs over the top of a high tree and lets himself fall from that eminence without any thought of saving his life and limbs.

183. The Yogis and Sannyâsins are like snakes. The snake never digs a hole for

Sri Ramakrishna.

itself, but it lives in the hole made by the mouse. When one hole becomes uninhabitable, it enters into another hole. So the Yogis and Sannyâsins make no houses for themselves. They pass their days in other men's houses—to-day in one house, to-morrow in another.

184. A sage and a god should never be visited empty-handed. However trifling the present may be, one should never fail to place something before these great ones.

"O Mother Divine! I want no honor from men, I want no pleasure of the flesh, only let my soul flow into Thee as the permanent confluence of the Ganges and the Jamuná. Mother, I am without Bhakti (devotion), without Yoga, I am poor and friendless. I want no one's praises, only let my mind always dwell in the lotus of Thy feet."

SPIRITUAL LIFE.

185. Every man should follow his Each
own religion. A Christian should follow should
Christianity, a Mahomedan should follow his own
Mahomedanism, and so on. For the religion.
Hindus the ancient path, the path of the
Aryan *Rishis*, is the best.

186. People partition off their lands by
means of boundaries, but no one can
partition off the all-embracing sky over-
head. The indivisible sky surrounds all
and includes all. So common man in
ignorance says, "My religion is the only
one, my religion is the best." But when
his heart is illumined by true knowledge,
he knows that above all these wars of
sects and sectarians presides the one indivisible, eternal, all-knowing Bliss.

187. As a mother, in nursing her sick
children, gives rice and curry to one, and
sago arrow-root to another and bread and

butter to a third, so the Lord has laid out different paths for different men suitable to their natures.

Tolerance for other religions. 188. A truly religious man should think that other religions also are paths leading to truth. We should always maintain an attitude of respect towards other religions.

189. Remain always strong and steadfast in thy own faith, but eschew all bigotry and intolerance.

190. Be not like the frog in the well. The frog in the well knows nothing bigger and grander than its own well. So are all bigots; they do not see anything better than their own creeds.

Avoid vain discussion. 191. Dispute not. As you rest firmly on your own faith and opinion, allow others also the equal liberty to stand by their own faiths and opinions. By mere disputation you will never succeed in convincing another of his error. When the grace of God descends on him, each one will understand his own mistakes.

Sri Ramakrishna.

192. To drink pure water from a shallow pond, one should gently take the water from the surface and not disturb it. If it is disturbed, the sediments will rise up from the bottom and make the whole water muddy. If you desire to be pure, have firm faith and slowly go on with your devotional practices, and waste not your energies in useless scriptural discussions and arguments. The little brain will otherwise be muddled.

193. So long as the bee is outside the petals of the lily, and has not tasted the sweetness of its honey, it hovers round the flower emitting its buzzing sound; but when it is inside the flower, it noiselessly drinks its nectar. So long as a man quarrels and disputes about doctrines and dogmas, he has not tasted the nectar of true faith; when he has tasted it, he becomes quiet and full of peace.

194. When water is poured into an empty vessel, a bubbling noise ensues, but when the vessel is full, no such noise is heard. Similarly the man who has not found God is full of vain disputations

about the existence and attributes of the Godhead. But he who has seen Him silently enjoys the bliss Divine.

Rites and ceremonies. 195. People of this age care for the essence of everything. They will accept the essential of religion and not its non-essentials (that is, the rituals, ceremonials, dogmas and creeds).

196. Although in a grain of paddy the germ is considered the only necessary thing (for germination and growth), while the husk or chaff is considered to be of no importance; still if the husked grain be put into the ground, it will not sprout up and grow into a plant and produce rice. To get a crop one must needs sow the grain with the husk on. But if one wants to get at the kernel itself, he must remove the husk of the grain. So rites and ceremonies are necessary for the growth and perpetuation of a religion. They are the receptacles that contain the kernel of truth, and consequently every man must perform them before he reaches the central truth.

Sri Ramakrishna.

197. Honor spirit and form, both sentiment within and symbol without.

198. The pearl oyster that contains the precious pearl is in itself of very little value, but it is essential for the growth of the pearl. The shell itself may prove to be of no use to the man who has got the pearl. So ceremonies and rites may not be necessary for him who has attained the Highest Truth—God.

199. Devotional practices are necessary only so long as tears of ecstasy do not flow at hearing the name of *Hari*. He needs no devotional practices whose heart is moved to tears at the mere mention of the name of *Hari*.

200. The soul reincarnates in a body of which it was thinking just before its last departure from this world. Devotional practices may therefore be seen to be very necessary. When by constant practice no worldly ideas arise in the mind, then the God-idea alone fills the soul and does not leave it even when on the brink of eternity.

201. *Q.* What is the difference between the Sâttwika, the Râjasika, and the Ta-masik's way of worship?

A. The man who worships from the depths of his heart, without pomp and vanity and without the idea of show, is a Sâttwika worshipper.

The man who decorates his house, has music and dance, and makes costly preparations for a rich feast of fruits and sweetmeats in celebrating the worship of the Deity, is a Râjasika worshipper.

The man who immolates hundreds of innocent goats and sheep on the altar, has dishes of meat and wine, and becomes absorbed in dancing and singing, is the Tamasika worshipper.

Sects.　202. *Q.* Is it good to create sects (Dal)? (Here is a pun on the word "Dal," which means both a "sect" as well as "the rank growth on the surface of a stagnant pool.")

A. The Dal cannot grow in a current of water: it grows only in the stagnant waters of small pools. He whose heart longs for the Deity has no time for anything else. He who looks for fame and honor forms sects (Dal).

Sri Ramakrishna.

203. Dala (sedge) does not grow in large and pure water-tanks but in small stagnant and miasmatic pools. Similarly, Dala (schism) does not take place in a party whose adherents are guided by pure, broad, and unselfish motives, but it takes firm root in a party whose advocates are given to selfishness, insincerity and bigotry. ("Dala" in Bengâli means both sedges and schism.)

204. Some years ago, when the Hindus and the Brâhmas were preaching their respective religions with true earnestness and great zeal, some one asked Bhagavân Srî Râmakrishna his opinion about the two parties, on which he replied, "I see that my Mother Divine is getting Her work done through both parties."

205. Q. There are various sects among the Hindus, which sect or creed should we adopt?
A. Pârvati once asked Mahâdeva, "O Lord! what is the root of the Eternal, Everlasting, All-embracing Bliss?" To her Mahâdeva replied, "The root is faith." So the peculiarities of creeds and sects

matter little or nothing. Let every one perform with faith the devotions and the duties of his own creed.

206. Questioned by a pious Brâhma as to the difference between Hinduism and Brâhmaism, the Bhagavân said: "It is like the difference between the single note of music and the whole music. The Brahmo religion is content with the single note of the Brahman, while the Hindu religion consists of several notes producing a sweet, melodious harmony."

207. *Q.* Why do religions degenerate?
A. The rain-water is pure but becomes soiled on earth according to the medium it passes through. If the roof and the pipes be dirty, the water discharged through them must also be dirty.

Easy to talk religion, difficult to act it.
208. It is easy to utter "do, re, mi, fa, sol, la, si," by mouth, but not so easy to sing or play them on any instrument. So it is easy to talk religion, but it is difficult to act religion.

209. Common men talk bagfuls of religion but act not a grain of it, while

the wise man speaks little, but his whole life is a religion acted out.

210. What you wish others to do, do yourself.

211. Man is born in this world with two tendencies—the Vidyâ tendency, or tendency towards liberation, and the Avidyâ tendency, or tendency towards world and bondage. When born, both tendencies are in equilibrium like the scales of a balance. The world soon places its enjoyments and pleasures in one scale, and the spirit its attractions on the other; and if the intellect chooses the world, the worldly scale becomes heavy and gravitates towards the earth. But if it chooses the spirit, the spiritual scale gravitates towards God. *Man born with two tendencies.*

212. Seeing the water pass glittering through a network of bamboo twigs, the small fry enter into it with great pleasure, and having once entered, they cannot get out and are caught. Similarly, foolish men enter into the world, allured by its false glitter, but as it is easier to enter

the net than to get out of it, so it is easier to enter the world than to renounce it, after having once entered it.

Direct young hearts towards God. 213. The tender bamboo can be easily bent, but the full-grown bamboo breaks when attempt is made to bend it. It is easy to bend young hearts towards God, but the heart of the old escapes the hold when so drawn.

214. A ripe mango may be offered to God, or to a sage, or may be used for other purposes; but if it be once picked into by a crow, it becomes unfit for all use. It can neither be offered to the Deity, nor given to a Brâhmin in charity, nor should it be eaten by any one. Similarly, boys and girls should be dedicated to the service of God when their hearts are pure and when the impurity of worldly desires has not tainted them. Let once worldly desires enter into their minds, or let the demon of sensual pleasures cast his baneful shadow over them, it is then very difficult to make them tread the path of virtue.

Sri Ramakrishna.

215. The new-born calf looks very lively, blithe, and merry. It jumps and runs all day long, and only stops to suck the sweet milk from its dam. But no sooner is the rope placed round its neck than it begins to pine away gradually, and, far from being merry, wears a dejected and sorry appearance, and gets almost reduced to a skeleton. So long as a boy has no concern with the affairs of the world, he is as merry as the day is long. But when he once feels the weight of responsibilities of a man of family, by binding himself in time to the world by the indissoluble tie of wedlock, then he no longer appears jolly, but wears the look of dejection, care, and anxiety, and is seen to lose the glow of health from his cheeks, while wrinkles gradually make their appearance on the forehead. Blessed is he that remains a boy throughout his life, free as the morning air, fresh as a newly-blown flower, and pure as a dew-drop.

216. *Q*. Why do you love young men? *A*. Because they possess the whole of their minds. One half the mind of a married man goes to his wife. When a child

is born, it takes away one fourth, and the remaining one fourth is scattered over relatives, friends, business, name, food, clothes, etc. Therefore a young mind can easily acquire God.

217. The parrot cannot be taught to sing if it becomes old and the membrane of its throat becomes hardened. It must be taught before the collar line appears and while it is young. So in old age it is difficult for the mind to be fixed on God. It can be easily done in youth.

The worldly find no opportunity to practice devotion. 218. A person said: "When my boy Harish grows up, I will get him married, and giving him the charge of the family, I shall renounce the world and begin to practise Yoga." At this the Bhagavân said: "You will never find any opportunity to practise Yoga (devotion). You will say afterwards, 'Harish and Girish are very much attached to me. They do not like to leave my company as yet.' Then you will desire, perhaps, 'Let Harish have a son, and let me see that son married.' Thus there will be no end of your desires."

84

Sri Ramakrishna.

219. The evil spirit is exorcised by throwing magnetized mustard seeds on the patient, but if the spirit has entered into the seed itself, how can such seed remove the evil spirit? If the mind with which thou art to contemplate the Deity be attached to the vicious thoughts of the world, how canst thou expect to do successfully thy religious devotions with such a corrupt instrument?

220. Worldly men repeat the name of *Hari* (God) and perform various pious and charitable deeds with the hope of worldly rewards, but when misfortune, sorrow, poverty, death approach them, they forget them all. They are like the parrot that repeats by rote the Divine name "Radha Krishna, Radha Krishna" the livelong day, but cries "Kaw, Kaw," when caught by a cat, forgetting the Divine name. *The worldly insincere in their professions of piety.*

221. A spring cushion is squeezed down when one sits upon it, but it soon resumes its original shape when the pressure is removed. So it is with worldly souls. They are full of religious sentiments and

in pious moods so long as they hear religious talks; but no sooner do they enter
into the daily routine of the world than
they forget all those high and noble
thoughts and become as impure as before.

222. So long as the iron is in the furnace
it is red hot, but it becomes black soon
after it is taken out. So is also the
worldly man. So long as he is in a
church, or in the society of pious people,
he is full of religious emotions, but no
sooner does he come out of those associations than he loses them all.

Religious advice unheeded by the worldly. 223. As the water enters in on one side
under a bridge and soon passes out on the
other, so religious advice enters into the
heart of a worldly man by one ear and
goes out by the other without making any
impression upon his mind.

224. As a nail cannot be driven into a
stone but can easily be driven into the
earth, so the advice of a sage does not
affect the soul of a worldly man; it enters
easily into the heart of a believer.

Sri Ramakrishna.

225. By talking with a worldly man one can feel that his heart is filled with worldly thoughts and desires even as the crop of a pigeon is filled with grains.

226. The characteristic of a thoroughly worldly man is that he does not only not listen to hymns, religious discourses, praises of the Almighty, etc., but also prevents others from hearing them, and abuses religious men and societies, and scoffs at prayers.

227. As a little boy or girl can have no idea of conjugal affection, even so a worldly man cannot at all comprehend the ecstasy of Divine Communion.

228. The alligator has such a thick and scaly skin that no weapon can pierce it. So, how much soever you may preach religion to a worldly man, it will have no effect upon his heart.

229. The heart of a sinner is like a Heart of curled hair. You may pull it ever so a sinner. long but will not succeed in making it

87

straight. So, also, the heart of the wicked cannot be easily changed.

230. As water does not enter into a stone, so religious advice produces no impression on the imprisoned soul or *Baddha Jiva*.

231. As sieves separate the finer and coarser parts of a pulverized or ground substance, keeping the coarser and rejecting the finer, even so the wicked man takes the evil and rejects the good.

232. A wicked man's mind is like the curly tail of a dog.

233. When the mind dwells in evil propensities it is like a high caste Brâhmin living in the quarters of the outcastes, or like a gentleman dwelling in the back slums of a town.

234. Let not thy mind be as the storehouse of a washerman. He fills his room with the unclean clothes of others, but when those clothes are clean and ready for use, they go to their respective owners and he has nothing to call his own.

Sri Ramakrishna.

235. The mind attached to lust and wealth is like the unripe betel-nut attached to its shell; so long as the betel-nut is not ripe, it remains fixed to its shell by its juice, but when the juicy substance dries by time, the nut becomes detached from its shell and is felt rolling inside the shell, if shaken. So when the juice of attachment to gold and lust is dried up, the man becomes free. **Mind attached to lust and wealth.**

236. As a soft clay easily takes an impression, but not the stone, so also the Divine Wisdom impresses itself on the heart of a devotee, but not on that of the bound soul.

237. A wet match does not ignite; however hard you may rub it, it only smokes. But a dry match catches fire at once, even with the slightest rubbing. The heart of the devotee is like the dry match; the slightest mention of the name of the Lord kindles the fire of love in his heart; but the mind of the worldly man soaked in lust and wealth is like the moist match. Though God may be preached a

number of times, the fire of love can never
be kindled in him.

Worldly men unchanged by Divine Grace. 238. When the Malaya breeze blows,
all trees having stamina in them become
converted into sandal-trees; but those
which have no stamina remain unchanged
as before, like bamboo, plantain, palm-
tree, &c. So when Divine Grace descends, men having the germs of piety
and goodness in them are changed at once
into holy beings and are filled with Divinity, but worthless and worldly men
remain as before.

239. Flies sit at times on the sweetmeats kept exposed for sale in the shop of
a confectioner; but no sooner does a
sweeper pass by with a basket full of filth
than the flies leave the sweetmeats and
sit upon the filth-basket. But the honey-
bee never sits on filthy objects, and always
drinks honey from the flowers. The
worldly men are like flies. At times they
get a momentary taste of Divine sweetness, but their natural tendency for filth
soon brings them back to the dunghill of
the world. The good man, on the other

hand, is always absorbed in the beatific contemplation of Divine Beauty.

N. B.—The worldly man is like a worm that always lives and dies in filth, and has no idea of higher things; the good man of the world is like the fly that sits now on the filth and now on the sweet; while the free soul of a Yogin is like the bee that always drinks the honey of God's holy presence, and nothing else.

240. The man immersed in worldliness cannot attain the knowledge Divine. He cannot see God. Does the muddy water ever reflect the sun or any surrounding object?

241. As the troubled surface of rolling waters does not reflect the full moon properly, but in broken images; so the mind that is disturbed by worldly desires and passions does not fully reflect the light of God.

242. Soft clay admits of forms, but the burnt clay does not. So those whose hearts are consumed with the fire of worldly desires cannot be impressed with higher ideas.

The Sayings of

**Teach-
ings of
the
Worldly.**
243. The cries of all jackals are alike.
The teachings of all the wise men of the
world are essentially one and the same.

244. The vulture soars high up in the
air, but all the time he is looking down
into the charnel-pits in search of putrid
carcases.   So the book-read pandits
speak glibly and volubly about Divine
Knowledge, but it is all mere talk, for all
the while their mind is thinking about
how to get money, respect, power, etc.,
the vain guerdon of their learning.

245. A worldly man may be endowed
with intellect as great as that of Janaka,
may take as much pains and trouble as a
Yogin, and make as great sacrifices as an
ascetic; but all these he makes and does,
not for God, but for worldliness, honor,
and wealth.

246. Of all the birds of the air the crow
is considered to be the wisest, and he
thinks himself so too.   He never falls into
a snare.   He flies off at the slightest approach of danger, and steals the food with
the greatest dexterity.   But all this wis-

92

Sri Ramakrishna.

dom can supply him with no better living
than filth and foul matter. This is the
result of his having the wisdom of the
pettifogger.

247. As the fly now sits on the unclean **Mind of**
sore of the human body and now on the **worldly**
offerings dedicated to the gods, so the **man.**
mind of the worldly man is at one time
engaged in religious topics and at the next
moment loses itself in the pleasures of
wealth and lust.

248. When a certain quantity of pure
milk is mixed with double the quantity
of water, it takes a long time and labor
to thicken it to the consistency of *kshira*
(condensed milk). The mind of a worldly
man is largely diluted with the water of
evil and impure thoughts and it requires
a long time and labor before anything can
be done to purify and give proper consistency to it.

249. If a man suffering from very high
fever and dying of thirst be placed near
pitchers filled with ice-cold water and a
set of open-mouthed bottles filled with

savory sauces, is it possible for such a
thirsty and restless patient to resist the
temptation of drinking the water or tasting the sauces? Similarly the worldly
man who is suffering from the high fever
of lust and is thirsty for sensual pleasures
cannot resist the temptations when he is
placed between the attractions of woman's
charm on the one side and those of wealth
on the other. He is sure to deviate from
the path of righteousness.

The worldly minded prefer sense pleasures. 250. The worldly-minded man prefers
the pleasures of the senses to the bliss of
Divine Communion. A certain worldly
disciple of the Bhagavân was once at his
request put into the state of Samâdhi by
the Bhagavân. Doctors could not bring
him out of that state and its intoxication
lasted fifteen days. On regaining consciousness by the touch of the Bhagavân,
the disciple said: "Lord, what shall I do
with this state now, my sons are not
capable of looking after my properties?"

251. None ventures to keep milk in an
earthen pot in which curd has once
formed, lest the milk itself should get

Sri Ramakrishna.

curdled. Nor can the vessel be safely used for other working purposes lest it should crack upon the fire. It is therefore almost useless. A good and experienced Guru (preceptor) does not entrust to a worldly man valuable and exalting precepts, for he is sure to misinterpret and misuse them to suit his own mean designs. Nor will he ask him to do any useful work that may cost a little labor, lest he should think that the preceptor was taking undue advantage of him.

252. As it is very difficult to gather the mustard seeds that escape out of a torn package and are scattered in all directions; so when the human mind runs in diverse directions and is occupied with many things in the world, it is not a very easy task to collect and concentrate it.

253. The heavier scale of a balance goes down while the lighter one rises up. Similarly he who is weighed down with too many cares and anxieties of the world goes down into it, while he who has fewer cares rises up towards the Kingdom of Heaven.

The Sayings of

254. *Q.* What is the world like?

A. It is like an Âmlâ fruit, all skin and stone with but very little pulp, the eating of which produces colic.

Salvation for worldly-minded in renunciation. 255. *Q.* What state of mind being attained to, can the worldly-minded get salvation?

A. If by the grace of God the quick spirit of renunciation come to one, then one can get rid of the attachment to lust and wealth and then only is one free from all worldly bondages.

256. When paper is moistened with oil it cannot be written upon. So the soul spoiled by the oil of sense-enjoyments is unfit for spiritual devotion. But just as oiled paper, when overlaid with chalk, can be written upon; so when the soul is chalked over with renunciation, it again becomes fit for spiritual progress.

257. The key to open that room wherein God is, works in a curiously contrary way. To reach God you have to renounce the world.

Sri Ramakrishna.

258. This world is like a stage where men perform many parts under various disguises. They do not like to take off the mask, unless they have played for some time. Let them play for a while, and then they will leave off the mask of their own accord.

259. Whatever gives enjoyment in this world contains a bit of divine happiness in it. The difference between the two is as between treacle and refined candy.

260. *Q.* The world and God, how is it possible to harmonize both?

A. Look to the carpenter's wife, how diversely busy she is! With one hand she is stirring the *cheera* (flattened rice) in the mortar of a *dhenki* (a wooden husking and rice-flattening machine), with the other she is holding the child to her breast and suckling it, and at the same time bargaining with a purchaser about the *cheera*. Thus, though manifold are her occupations, her mind is fixed on the one idea that the pestle of the *dhenki* shall not fall on her hand and bruise it. Be in the

How to harmonize world and God.

world, but always remember Him and never go astray from His path.

261. As the street minstrel with one hand plays upon the guitar and with the other strikes a drum, all the while chanting a song; so, O thou world-bound soul, perform all thy worldly duties with thy hands, but never forget to repeat and glorify the name of the Lord with all thy heart.

262. As persons living in a house infested by venomous snakes are always alert and cautious, so should men living in the world be always on their guard against the allurements of lust and greed.

How to conquer Passions. 263. On being asked when the enemies, lust, anger, etc., can be vanquished, the Bhagavân replied: So long as these passions are directed towards the world and its objects, they are enemies; but when they are directed towards the Deity, they become the best friends of man, for they take him to the Godhead. Lust for worldly things must be changed to lust for God; the anger which you feel towards your fellow-creatures must be directed towards God for not manifesting Himself to you, and so on with all your passions. The passions should not be eradicated but educated.

264. The snake is very venomous; it bites when any one approaches it to catch it. But the person who has learned the art of snake-charming can not only catch a snake, but carries about several of them hanging round his neck and arms like so many ornaments. Similarly, he who has acquired spiritual knowledge can never be polluted by lust and greed. **Saving Power of Divine Wisdom.**

265. Unshod and with bare feet who will venture to walk upon thorns and sharp stones? Shod with Divine wisdom (Tattwajnana) what thorn or sharp stone can harm you?

266. If you first smear the palms of your hands with oil and then break open the jack-fruit, the sticky milky exudation of the fruit will not stick to the hands and thus trouble you. So if you first fortify yourself with the true knowledge of the

Universal Self and then live in the midst
of wealth and women they will affect you
in no way.

267. "Fastening in thy garment the
knowledge of Advaita (one-ness or non-
duality) do whatever thou wishest."

Good and evil cannot bind him who has
realized the oneness of the nature and Self
with the Brahman.

First seek God, then the world. 268. To some one the Bhagavân said:
Well, now you have come to seek God
when you have spent the greater part of
your life in the world. Had you entered
the world after realizing God, what peace
and joy you would have found!

269. First gain God and then gain
Wealth, but do not do the contrary. If
after acquiring spirituality you lead a
worldly life, then you will never lose your
peace of mind.

270. As a boy holding on to a post or a
pillar gyrates round it with headlong speed
without fear of falling; so, fixing thy hold

Sri Ramakrishna.

firmly on God, perform thy worldly duties, and thou shalt be free from all dangers.

271. Do not let worldly thoughts and anxieties disturb your mind. Do everything that is necessary in its proper time and let your mind be always fixed on God.

272. As an unchaste woman, busily engaged in household affairs, is all the while thinking of her secret lover, even so, O thou man of the world, do thy round of worldly duties, but fix thy heart always on the Lord.

273. A husbandman was watering a sugar-cane field the whole of a day. After finishing his task he saw that not a drop of water had entered the field; all the water had gone underground through several big rat-holes. Such is the state of that devotee who, cherishing secretly in his heart worldly desires (of fame, pleasures, and comforts) and ambitions, worships God. Though daily praying, he makes no progress because his entire devotion runs to waste through the rat-holes of these desires, and at the end of

The devotee who cherishes worldly desires.

his life-long devotion he is the same man as before, and has not advanced a bit.

274. He who is a thief of his own thoughts does not accomplish anything. How canst thou see God when thy whole heart and soul do not long for Him?

275. What you think, you should say. Let there be a harmony between your thoughts and words; otherwise, if you merely tell that God is your All-in-All, while your mind has made the world its All-in-All, you cannot derive any benefit thereby.

276. A boat may stay in the water, but the water should not stay in the boat. An aspirant may live in the world, but the world should not live in him.

277. If there is a small hole in the bottom of a jar of water, the whole water flows out of it by that small aperture. Similarly if there be the slightest tinge of worldliness in the neophyte, all his exertions come to naught.

Sri Ramakrishna.

278. So long as the fire is beneath, the milk boils and bubbles. Remove the fire and it is quiet again. Similarly the heart of the neophyte boils with enthusiasm so long as he goes on with his spiritual exercises, but afterwards it cools down.

279. Milk and water when brought into contact are sure to mix, so that the milk can never be kept separated again. Similarly if the neophyte, thirsting after self-improvement, mixes indiscriminately with all sorts of worldly people, not only does he lose his ideal, but also his former faith, love and enthusiasm die away imperceptibly.

Neophite must not mix with the worldly.

280. When butter is produced by churning the whey, it should not be kept in the same vessel containing the remaining whey, for then it will lose some of its sweetness and cohesion. It should be kept in pure water and in a different vessel. So after attaining some partial perfection in this world, if a man still continues to mix with the worldly and remains in the midst of the world, it is likely

that he will be tainted; but he will remain
pure if he lives out of it.

281. You cannot live in a sooty room
without blackening your body to some
extent, however small it may be, with all
your caution. So, if a man or woman
lives in the company of one of the oppo-
site sex of the same age with the greatest
circumspection and control over his or her
passion, still some carnality, however
small, is sure to arise in his or her mind.

**Avoid
wicked
Associ-
ation.**
282. It is true that God is even in the
tiger, but we must not go and face the
animal. So it is true that God dwells
even in the most wicked, but it is not
meet that we should associate with the
wicked.

283. Visit not miracle-workers. They
are wanderers from the path of truth.
Their minds have become entangled in
the meshes of psychic powers, which lie
in the way of pilgrims towards Brahman
as temptations. Beware of these powers
and desire them not.

Sri Ramakrishna.

284. All water is brooded over by Nârâyaṇa (Supreme Spirit), but every kind of water is not fit to drink. Similarly, though it is true that the Almighty dwells in every place, yet every place is not fit to be visited by man. As one kind of water may be used for washing our feet, another may serve the purposes of ablution, and others may be drunk, while others again may not be touched at all; so there are different kinds of places. We may approach some, we may enter into the inside of others, while others we must avoid even at a distance.

285. A young plant should be always protected by a fence from the mischief of goats and cows and little urchins. But when once it becomes a big tree, a flock of goats or a herd of cows may find shelter under its spreading boughs, and fill their stomachs with its leaves. So when you have but little faith within you, you should protect it from the evil influences of bad company and worldliness. But when once you grow strong in faith, no worldliness or evil inclination will dare approach your holy presence; and many

who are wicked will become godly through your holy contact.

Neophite should seek solitude and stillness. 286. Once some Brahmo boys told me that they followed Janaka's example; they lived in this world quite unattached to it. I said to them that it was easy *to say* that, but it was a different matter *to be* Janaka. It was so hard to move among worldly affairs without being contaminated. What terrible austerities did not Janaka practise at the outset! But I do not advise you to go through similar hardships, but what I do want you to do is to practise some devotion and to live alone for a time in some quiet place. Enter into the world after gaining Jnâna and Bhakti for yourselves. The best curd is formed when milk is left alone to stand quite still. The shaking or changing of pots spoils it. Janaka was unattached, hence one of the epithets applied to him was Videha (*literally*, body-less). He led the life of a Jivanmukta (*literally*, free though alive in the body); the annihilation of the body idea is exceedingly difficult to accomplish. Truly Janaka was a great hero. He handled with ease the two

Sri Ramakrishna.

swords—the one of Jnâna, and the other
of Karma.

287. If you have a mind to live unattached from the world, you should first
practise devotion in solitude for some
time,—say a year, or six months, or a
month, or at least twelve days. During
the period of retirement you should meditate constantly upon God and pray to Him
for Divine Love. You should revolve in
your mind the thought that there is nothing in the world that you may call your
own; those whom you think your own
will pass away in no time. God is really
your own, He is your All-in-All. How
to obtain Him should be your only concern.

288. Keep thyself aloof at the time of
thy devotions from those who scoff at
them and from those who ridicule piety
and the pious.

289. Keep thine own sentiments and
faith to thyself. Do not talk about them
abroad. Otherwise thou wilt be a great
loser.

The Sayings of

290. If you wash well the body of an elephant and let him at large, he is sure to get himself dirtied in no time; but if after washing him, you tie him down to his own room, he will remain clean. So if by the good influences of holy men you once become pure in spirit and then allow yourself to mix freely with worldly men, you are sure to lose that purity soon; but if you keep your mind fixed on God, you will never more get soiled in spirit.

The pure in heart see God. 291. The soiled mirror never reflects the rays of the sun, and the impure and unclean in heart who are subject to Mâyâ never perceive the glory of the Lord. But the pure in heart see the Lord as the clear mirror reflects the sun. Be holy, then.

292. As a man standing on the brink of a deep well is always afraid and watchful lest he fall into it, so should a man living in the world be always on his guard against temptations. He who has once fallen into the well of temptation can hardly come out of it pure and stainless.

Sri Ramakrishna.

293. That man, who living in the midst of the temptations of the world attains perfection, is the true hero.

294. The new-born calf feels unsteady and tumbles down scores of times before it learns to stand steady. So in the path of devotion the footslips are many and frequent before success is finally achieved.

295. The truly religious man is he who does not commit any sin even when he is alone, because God sees him, though no man may see him. He who can resist the temptation of lust and gold in a lonely place unobserved by any man, through the fear that God sees him, and who through such fear does not even think an evil thought, is truly a religious man. But he who practises religion for the sake of show and through the fear of public opinion has no religion in him. *The truly religious.*

296. Sin, like quicksilver, can never be concealed.

297. He is truly a pious man who is dead even in this life, i.e., whose pas-

sions and desires have been destroyed as
in a dead body.

298. As Heloncha (Hingcha repens)
should not be counted among pot-herbs
or sugar-candy among common sweets,
because even a sick man can use them.
without injuring his health; or as the
Pranava is not to be counted as a word,
but as Divinity itself; so the desires of
holiness, devotion, and love are not to
be reckoned as desires at all.

299. Sugar and sand may be mixed together, but the ant rejects the sand and
goes off with the sugar-grain; so pious
men sift the good from the bad.

300. It is the nature of the winnowing
basket to reject the bad and keep the
good; even such is the case with pious
men.

301. *Q*. When does the attraction of
sensual and worldly pleasures die away?
A. In God, who is Indivisible Ever-
Existing Bliss, there is a consolidation
of all happiness and of all pleasures.

Sri Ramakrishna.

They who enjoy Him can find no attraction in the cheap and worthless pleasures of the world.

302. When the tail of the tadpole drops off, it can live both in water and on land. When the tail of ignorance drops off, man becomes free. He can then live both in God and in the world equally well.

303. Those who live in the world and Ascetics. try to find salvation are like soldiers that fight protected by the breastwork of a fort, while the ascetics who renounce the world in search of God are like soldiers fighting in the open field. To fight from within the fort is more convenient and safer than to fight in the open field.

304. Of the grains of paddy which are fried in a frying-pan, those few which leap out of the pan and burst outside are the best fried, being without the least mark of any tinge; every one of even the properly-fried grains in the pan itself is sure to have at least a very small charred mark of a burn. So of all good devotees, the few who altogether give up

111

the world and go out of it are perfect
without any spot, while even the best
devotees who are in the world must have
at least some small spot of imperfection
in their character.

305. *Q.* What is the nature of the ascetic
who has renounced the world, not through
conviction, but through feelings of tem-
porary disgust?

A. A man who has become an ascetic
owing to some misunderstanding with
his father, mother, or his wife, is called
an ascetic by disgust. His asceticism is
ephemeral and it is lost as soon as he gets
some fat appointment in a foreign land.
That man is sure to return to the bosom
of his family with accumulation of wealth
and riches.

306. If a white cloth is stained with a
small speck, the blackness appears very
ugly indeed by contrast; so the smallest
fault of a holy man becomes painfully
prominent by his surrounding purity.

307. As by rubbing gold and brass on
a touchstone one tests the quality of the

Sri Ramakrishna.

metal, so the sincere Sâdhu (holy one) and a hypocrite are found out when they are rubbed on the touchstone of persecution and adversity.

308. The Sâdhu who distributes medicines and uses intoxicants is not a proper Sâdhu; avoid the company of such.

309. Out of the myriads of paper kites that are made to fly in the air, only one or two rend the string and get free. So out of hundreds of Sâdhakas (seekers after freedom) only one or two get free from this worldly bondage.

310. As when fishes are caught in a net, some do not struggle at all but remain calm in the net, some again struggle hard to come out of the net, while a few are very happy to effect their escape by rending the net; so there are three sorts of men—fettered (Baddha), struggling (Mumukshu), and released (Mukta).

311. When an unbaked pot is broken, the potter can use its clay to make a new pot; but when a baked pot is broken, he

does not use its pieces any longer. So, when a person dies in a state of ignorance, he must be born again; but when he becomes well baked in the fire of true knowledge, i.e., when he becomes perfect, he is not born again after death.

312. The boiled paddy grain does not grow again. Only the unboiled paddy grain brings forth the shoot. Similarly when a man dies becoming perfect (Siddha), he has not to be born again; but an imperfect man (Asiddha) has to be born again and again until he becomes a Siddha.

313. There are two classes of people who attain perfection in this world: those who get the truth and become silent, enjoying it all to themselves without any thought of others; people of the other class get the truth and cannot find pleasure in keeping it to themselves, but cry out in a trumpet voice to all, "Come ye and enjoy the truth with us."

314. There are three dolls, the first made of salt, the second made of cloth, and the third made of stone. If these dolls be

Sri Ramakrishna.

immersed in water, the first will get dissolved and lose its form, the second will absorb a large quantity of water and retain its form, while the third will be impervious to the water. The first doll represents the man who merges his self in the universal and all-pervading Self and becomes one with It; that is a Muktapurusha. The second represents a true lover or Bhakta, who is full of Divine bliss and knowledge; and the third represents a worldly man who will not admit even the least trace of true knowledge within.

315. The coverings of cakes are made of rice flour, but they are stuffed inside with different ingredients. The goodness or badness of the cake depends upon the quality of its stuffing. So all human bodies are made of one and the same material; but men are different in quality according to the purity of their hearts.

316. The spiritual gain of a person depends upon his sentiments and ideas, proceeds from his heart and not from his visible actions. Two friends while

Spiritual gain depends on heart.

strolling about, happened to pass by a
place where Bhâgavat (the word of God)
was being preached. One of them said:
"Brother, let us go there for a while and
hear the good words spoken." The other
replied, "No, friend, what is the use of
hearing the Bhâgavatam? Let us spend
the time in yonder public-house in amuse-
ment and pleasure." The first one did
not consent to this. He went to the place
where the Bhâgavatam was being read
and began to hear it. The other went to
the public-house, but did not find the
pleasure that he had anticipated there
and was thinking all the while, "Alas me!
Why have I come here? How happy is
my friend hearing all the while the sacred
life and deeds of *Hari* (Lord)." Thus
he meditated on *Hari* even though in a
public-house. The other man who was
hearing the Bhâgavatam, also did not find
pleasure in it. Sitting there, he began to
blame himself, saying, "Alas! Why did I
not accompany my friend to the public-
house? What a great pleasure he must
be enjoying at this time there!" The
result was that he who was sitting where
the Bhâgavatam was preached, meditated

on the pleasure of the public-house and acquired the fruit of the sin of going to the public-house because of his bad thoughts; while the man who had gone to the public-house acquired the merit of hearing the Bhâgavatam because of his good heart.

317. It is the mind that makes one wise or ignorant, bound or emancipated. One is holy because of his mind, one is wicked because of his mind, one is a sinner because of his mind, and it is the mind that makes one virtuous. So he whose mind is always fixed on God requires no other practices, devotion, or spiritual exercises.

Power of mind and thought.

318. The faith-healers of India order their patients to repeat with full conviction the words, "There is no illness in me, there is no illness at all." The patient repeats it, and thus mentally denying the illness goes off. So if you think yourself mortally weak, sinful and without goodness, you will really find yourself to be so in time. Know and believe that

you are of immense power and the power will come to you at last.

319. Many with a show of humility say, " I am like a low worm grovelling in the dust"; thus always thinking themselves worms, in time they become weak in spirit like worms. Let not despondency ever enter into thy heart; despair is the great enemy of progress in one's path. As a man thinketh, so he becometh.

320. A man sitting under the shade of the Kalpa-vriksha (wishing tree) wished to be a king and instantly he was a king. The next moment he wished to have a charming damsel and the damsel was instantly by his side. The man then thought to himself, " If a tiger should come and devour me!" and, alas! in an instant he was in the jaws of the tiger! God is like the wishing-tree: whosoever in His presence thinks that he is destitute and poor, remains as such; but he who believes that the Lord fulfils all his wants, receives everything from Him.

321. He who thinks that he is a Jiva (imperfect and worldly soul) is verily a

Jiva; he who considers himself to be God, verily becomes God. As one thinks, so he becomes.

322. When an elephant is let loose, it goes about uprooting trees and shrubs, but as soon as the driver pricks him on the head with the goad, he becomes quiet; so the mind, when unrestrained, wantons in the luxuriance of idle thoughts. but becomes at once calm when struck with the goad of right discrimination (Viveka).

323. A shy horse does not go straight so long as his eyes are not covered by blinders. Similarly the mind of a worldly man should be prevented from looking about by the blinders of Discrimination (Viveka) and Dispassion (Vairâgya), for then it will not stumble or go astray in evil paths.

Discrimination and Dispassion.

324. If you put any purifying substance, like a piece of alum, into a vessel of muddy water, the water is purified, and the impurities settle down at the bottom. Viveka (discrimination of the Real, God, from the unreal, phenomenal appear-

ances) and Vairâgya (non-attachment to the world) are the two purifiers of the human heart. With their help the mind of the worldly man ceases to be worldly and becomes pure.

325. The caterpillar gets itself imprisoned in its cell of self-woven cocoon. So the worldly soul gets itself entangled in the meshes of its desires. But when the caterpillar develops into a bright and beautiful butterfly, it rends the cocoon and enjoys freedom. So the worldly soul can be free from the meshes of Mâyâ by developing the wings of Viveka (discrimination) and Vairâgya (renunciation).

326. We must dive deep into the ocean of the Eternal-Intelligent-Bliss. Fear not the deep-sea monsters Avarice and Anger. Coat thyself with the turmeric of Discrimination and Dispassion (Viveka and Vairâgya) and those alligators will not approach thee, as the scent of this turmeric is too much for them.

327. Right discrimination is of two kinds—analytical and synthetical. The

Sri Ramakrishna.

first leads one from the phenomena to the Absolute Brahman, while by the second one knows how the Absolute Brahman appears in the universe.

328. *Q.* How many kinds of Vairâgya (renunciation) are there?

A. Generally there are two—the intense and the moderate. The intense Vairâgya is like digging a large tank in one night and filling it with water. The moderate renunciation is ever procrastinating. There is no knowing when it will become complete.

329. *Q.* How should one practise renunciation (Vairâgya)?

A. A wife once spoke to her husband, saying, "My dear, I am very anxious about my brother. For the last few days he has been thinking of renouncing the world and of becoming a Sannyâsin, and has begun preparations for it. He has been trying gradually to curb his desires and reduce his wants." The husband replied, "You need not be anxious about your brother. He will never become a Sannyâsin. No one has ever renounced

the world by making long preparations."
The wife asked, "How then does one become a Sannyâsin?" The husband answered, "Do you wish to see how one
renounces the world? Let me show you."
Saying this, instantly he tore his flowing
dress into pieces, tied one piece round his
loins, told his wife that she and all women
were henceforth his mother, and left the
house never to return.

Reading of the Scriptures. 330. It is useless to pore over holy
Scriptures and sacred Shastras without
a discriminating and dispassionate mind.
No spiritual progress can be made without
discrimination (Viveka) and renunciation
(Vairâgya).

331. "Grantha" does not always mean
a holy scripture, but it rather means a
"Granthi" or a knot. If a man does not
read it with an intense desire to know the
truth by renouncing all vanity, and even
his comforts, if that be necessary, mere
reading will breed in him pedantry, pre-
sumptuousness, egotism, etc., which re-
semble so many knots in his mind.

Sri Ramakrishna.

332. Those who have read a little become puffed up with pride. I had a conversation on God with ——. He said, "Oh, I know all these things." I said to him, "Does one who went to Delhi go about telling that he did so and make a display? Does a Babu say he is a Babu?"

333. The following are among those who cannot gain self-knowledge. Those who boast of learning, those who are proud of knowledge, and those who are vain of riches. If one says to these, "In such and such a place there is a good Sannyâsin, will you come to see him?" they will invariably make some excuses and say that they cannot go; but in their minds they think they are men of high positions, why should they go to another?

Those who cannot gain self-knowledge.

334. A well-known Brâhmo preacher said that the Paramahamsa was a madman and that his brain had got unsettled by constantly thinking upon one subject. The Paramahamsa, addressing the preacher, said, "Thou sayest that even in Europe learned men become mad by constantly thinking over one subject. But

what is that subject, matter or spirit? What wonder that a man should become mad by constantly thinking over matter! But how can one lose one's intelligence and become mad by thinking over that Intelligence from which the whole universe is made intelligent? Do thy scriptures teach thee so?"

Relative and absolute knowledge. 335. The eternal should be preached through the non-eternal, the real through the help of the unreal, and the noumena through the help of the phenomena.

336. When a sharp thorn finds its way into the sole of one's foot, one takes the help of another thorn to get the former out, and then casts both of them away. So relative knowledge (Vidyâ) alone can remove the relative ignorance (Avidyâ) which blinds the eye of Self. As both such knowledge and ignorance are comprised truly under Nescience, the man who attains the highest Jnâna or the knowledge of the Absolute does away with both Vidyâ and Avidyâ in the end, being himself free from all duality.

Sri Ramakrishna.

337. If you can detect and find out the universal illusion of Mâyâ, it will fly away from you just as a thief runs away when found out.

338. If the person possessed by the evil spirit has the consciousness that he is so possessed, the evil spirit at once leaves him. Similarly, the Jiva (individual soul) possessed by the spirit of Mâyâ (self-delusion) on realizing that he is self-deluded becomes at once free from Mâyâ.

339. There are people who, although they have nothing to attract them in this world, create some attachments for themselves and so try to bind themselves to this earth. They do not want and do not like to be free. A man who has no family to care for, no relatives to look after, generally takes a cat or a monkey or a dog or a bird for a pet object and companion, and thus slakes his thirst for milk by drinking mere whey. Such is the illusive power of Mâyâ over humanity.

340. A patient in high fever and excess of thirst imagines that he can drink away

quite a sea of water; but when that fit of fever goes and he regains his normal temperature, he can barely quaff off a single cupful of water, and his thirst is at once appeased with even a very small quantity of it. So a man, being under the feverish excitement of Mâyâ and forgetful of his own littleness, imagines that he can embrace the whole of Divinity within his own bosom, but when the illusion passes away, a single ray of Divine Light is seen to be sufficient to flood him with eternal Divine bliss.

341. Paramahamsa Deva once told a professional debater, "If you want to understand the Truth by arguing, then go to the Brahmo preacher K.; but if you want to understand it in a single word, then come to me."

Unreality of Universe. 342. An earnest seeker asked Him, "Kindly instruct me in one word so that I may be illumined." To which He replied, "Brahman is Truth and the Universe is unreal" (Brahmasatyam Jaganmithyâ).

Sri Ramakrishna.

343. A holy man used to look at a chandelier prism day and night and smile. The reason of his so doing was that he used to see various colors through the prism, red, yellow, etc., and as all these colors were false, so he knew the world to be unreal.

344. *Q.* Is this world unreal?

A. It is unreal so long as you do not know God. For you do not see Him (in everything) but fasten yourself to the world with the tie of "me and mine." Being thus deluded by ignorance, you become attached to sense objects and go deeper and deeper into the abyss of Mâyâ. Mâyâ makes men so utterly blind that they cannot get out of Samsâra (worldliness) even when the way lies straight open. You yourself know how unreal the Samsâra is. Think a little of the very house that we are in. How many men have been born and have died in it! Things of the world appear before us at one moment and vanish away at the next. Those whom you know to be your "own" will cease to exist for you the moment you close your eyes in death. How strong is the hold of attachment upon a worldly man! There is none in the family who requires his attention, yet for the sake of a grandson he cannot go to Benâres (to practise devotion). "What will become of my Haru?" is the one thought that keeps him bound to the world. In a *ghuni* (a trap for catching fish) the way out is always open, yet the fish do not get out of it. The caterpillar shuts itself up in its own saliva and perishes. Such Samsâra is undoubtedly unreal and evanescent.

The body transient. 345. *Q.* How may we conquer the love of life?

A. The human frame is made up of decaying things, of flesh, blood, bone, etc. It is a collection of flesh, bone, marrow, blood and other filthy substances subject to putrefaction. By thus analyzing the body, our love thereof vanishes.

346. No longer does one care for the cage when the bird has flown away from it. So when the bird of life flies away no one cares any longer for the carcass.

Sri Ramakrishna.

347. Disease is the tax which the soul pays for the use of the body, as the tenant pays house-tax for the house he occupies.

348. The body is transient and unimportant. Why then is it so much looked after? No one cares for an empty box. But people carefully preserve the box that contains money and other valuable property. The virtuous cannot but take care of the body, the temple of the soul in which God has manifested Himself, or which has been blessed by God's advent.

349. Q. How does the Lord dwell in the body?
A. He dwells in the body like the plug of a syringe—that is, in the body, and yet apart from it.

350. The human body is like a boiling pot, and the mind and the senses are like water, rice, potato, etc., in it. Put the pot with its ingredients on the fire, it will be so hot as to burn your finger when you touch it. But the heat does not belong to the pot, nor to anything contained in it, but is in the fire. So it is the fire of

Brahman in man that causes the mind and the senses to perform their functions, and when that fire ceases to act, the senses as well as the organs stop their functions.

Food and drink. 351. He cannot bestow any thought on such trifling questions as of food and drink whose mind yearns after God.

352. He who eats the food of the gods, namely, simple non-stimulating vegetable food, but does not desire to attain God, for him that simple food is as bad as beef. But he who eats beef and desires God, for him beef is as good as the food of the gods.

353. That is the truly prescribed diet (helpful to spirituality) which does not make the mind unsteady.

Money and riches. 354. Money can procure only bread and butter. Do not consider it therefore to be thy flesh and blood or thy sole end and aim.

355. There is nothing to be proud of in money. If you say that you are rich,

there are richer and richer men than you, in comparison with whom you are a mere beggar. After dusk, when the glow-worms make their appearance, they think, "We are giving light to the world." But when the stars rise, their pride is gone. Then the stars begin to think, "We are shedding light on the universe." After some time the moon ascends the sky, and the stars are humiliated and look melancholy. So again the moon begins to be proud and think that by her light the world is lighted, and smiles and bathes in beauty and cheerfulness. But lo! the dawn proclaims the advent of the rising sun on the eastern horizon. Where is the moon now? If they who think themselves rich ponder over these natural facts, they will never, never boast of their riches again.

356. He is the true man whose servant is money. Those who do not know how to use money do not deserve to be called men.

357. As water passes under a bridge but never stagnates, so money passes

through the hands of "The Free" who never hoard it.

Praise and censure. 358. One who spends his time in discussing the good and bad qualities of others wastes his time. For it is time spent neither in thinking about his own self nor of the Supreme Self, but of other selves.

359. Be indifferent to the praise and censure of mankind, considering them to be like the cawing of crows.

360. Men are quick to praise and quick to blame, so do not take to heart what others say of thee.

Forbearance and forgiveness. 361. In the Bengâli alphabet no three letters are alike in sound except the three sibilants (Sa, Sha, and sa), all meaning "forbear," "forbear," "forbear." This shows that even from our childhood we are made to learn forbearance in our very alphabets. The quality of forbearance is of the highest importance to every man.

362. The true character of the holy ones is all forgiveness.

Sri Ramakrishna.

363. The anger of the good is like a line which is formed on the surface of the water and which soon disappears.

364. As thieves cannot enter a house the inmates of which are wide awake, so if you are always on your guard, no evil desires will be able to enter your heart to rob it of its goodness.

365. *Q.* How long does godliness remain in man?
A. Iron is red so long as it is in the fire. It is black the moment that it is removed from fire. So the human being is godly so long as he is in communion with God.

366. *Q.* When does a man get salvation? **Egoism.**
A. When his egoism dies.

367. So long as there is egoism, neither self-knowledge (Jnâna) nor liberation (Mukti) is possible and no cessation of births and deaths.

368. The sun can give heat and light to the whole world, but he can do nothing when the clouds are in the sky and shut

133

out his rays. Similarly, so long as the cloud of egoism is in the soul the light of God does not shine upon it.

369. Egoism is like a cloud that keeps God hidden from our sight. If by the mercy of the Guru egoism vanishes, God is seen in His full glory. As, for instance, you see in the picture that Sri Râmachandra, who is God, is only two or three steps ahead of Lakshman (the Jiva or individual soul), but Sita (Mâyâ), coming in between the two, prevents Lakshman from having a view of Râma.

370. If I hold up this cloth before me, you will not see me any more, though I shall be as near you. So also God is nearer to you than anything else, yet because of the screen of egoism you cannot see Him.

371. Q. Sir, why are we so bound? Why can we not see God?
A. Egoism is the Mâyâ for the Jiva. Egoism shuts the light out. When "I" will die, all trouble will cease. If by the grace of God the idea of "I am the non-doer" is firmly settled in the heart, a man be-

comes free even in this life and there is
no more fear for him.

372. Those who seek for fame are under **The de-**
delusion. They forget that everything **luded say,**
is ordained by the Great Disposer of all **"It is I."**
things,—the Supreme Being, and that all
is due to the Lord and to no one else. It
is the wise who say always, "It is Thou,
It is Thou, O Lord," but the ignorant
and the deluded say, "It is I, It is I."

373. So long as you say "I know" or
"I do not know," you look upon your-
self as a person. My Divine Mother says:
"It is only when I efface all Aham
(I-ness) in you that the Undifferentiated
(My impersonal aspect) may be realized
in Samâdhi." Till then there is the "I"
in me and before me.

374. Sankarâchârya had a disciple who
served him for a long time, but he did not
give any instructions to him. Once
when Sankara was seated alone, he heard
the footsteps of some one coming behind. He called out, "Who is there?"
The disciple answered, "It is I." The

The Sayings of

Âchârya said, "If the word 'I' is so dear to thee, then either expand it indefinitely, that is, know the universe as thyself, or renounce it altogether."

How to destroy egoism. 375. *Q.* How can the idea of egohood be destroyed?

A. It requires constant practice to do it. In threshing out rice from the paddy, one must look to it from time to time to see that the rice is properly husked; if not, one must of course go on threshing.

376. In making delicate weighments one has to shake the balance from time to time to see whether the oscillating needle will every time come back to the middle point; if it does not do so, the weighment is incorrect. Similarly a man must test himself from time to time to see whether he has conquered his lower self.

377. The dyspeptic knows too well that sour stuffs are injurious to him, but such is the force of association that their sight is enough to make his mouth water. So, even if one tries hard to suppress the

136

Sri Ramakrishna.

idea of I-ness and mine-ness, yet in the field of action his unripe ego shows itself.

378. If you find that you cannot make this "I" go, then let it remain as the "servant I." There is not much to fear of mischief in the "I" which knows itself as "I am the servant of God; I am His devotee." Sweets beget dyspepsia, but the crystallized sugar candy is not among the sweets for it has not that injurious property.

Ego as servant of God.

379. The "servant I," the "I" of a devotee, or the "I" of a child is like the line drawn with a stick on a sheet of water. It does not last long.

380. If one ponders over the "I," and tries to find out what it is, one sees it is only a word which denotes egoism. It is extremely difficult to shake off. Then one says, "You wicked 'I,' if you will not go by any means, remain as the servant of God." This is called the "ripe I."

381. If you feel proud, feel so in the thought that you are the servant of God,

the son of God. Great men have the nature of children. They are always children before God, so they have no egoism. All their strength is of God, belonging to and coming from Him, nothing of themselves.

Self-will merged in Divine will. 382. If one acquires the conviction that everything is done by God's will, that one is only the tool in the hands of God, then is one free even in this life. "Thou doest Thy work, they say, 'I do it !'"

383. Freedom will come when thy I-hood (egoism) will vanish and thy self-will be merged in the Divinity.

384. The true nature of the Jiva (individual soul) is eternal Existence-Knowledge-Bliss. It is egoism that has brought about so many upâdhis (limitations), and he has forgotten his own nature.

385. Know thyself and thou shalt then know the non-self and the Lord of all. What is my ego? Is it my hand or foot, or flesh or blood, or muscle or tendon?

Sri Ramakrishna.

Ponder deep and thou shalt know that there is no such thing as " I." As by con-tinually peeling off the skin of an onion, so on analyzing the ego it will be found that there is not any real entity corre-sponding to the ego. The ultimate result of all such analysis is God. When ego-ism drops away Divinity manifests itself.

386. *Q*. Will egoism never die off fully? **Will egoism die fully?**
A. The petals of the lotus drop off in time but they leave the scars behind them. So the egoism of man does go off entirely, but the traces of its former existence remain. They, however, are not at all active for evil.

387. The cup in which garlic juice is kept retains the nasty odor though it may be rubbed and scoured hundreds of times. Egohood also is such an obstinate creature that it never leaves us completely.

388. The leaves of the cocoa-palm fall off, but leave their marks behind on the trunk. Similarly, so long as one has his body, there will remain the mark of ego-ism, how high soever a man may advance

in spirituality. But these traces of egoism do not bind such men to the world or cause their rebirth.

Two Egos. 389. There are two egos—one ripe and the other unripe. "Nothing is mine; whatever I see, feel or hear, nay, even this body, is not mine. I am always eternal, free, and all-knowing"—the ego that has this idea is the ripe one, while the unripe ego is that which thinks, "This is my house, my child, my wife, my body, etc."

390. The ego of the servant, the ego of the devotee—the ego of Vidya—these are the names of the ripe ego.

391. *Q.* What is called the "mischievous I"?

A. The "I" which says, "Don't they know me? I have so much money, who is so wealthy as myself? Who dares surpass me?"

392. The nature of *Tamas* is egoism which is bred of ignorance.

393. When shall I be free? When the "I" has vanished. "I and mine" is

Sri Ramakrishna.

ignorance; "Thou and Thine" is true **All be-**
knowledge. The true devotee always **longs to**
says, "O Lord, Thou art the doer (Kartâ), **God.**
Thou doest everything. I am only a
machine. I do whatever Thou makest
me to do. And all this is Thy glory.
This home and this family are Thine, not
mine; I have only the right to serve as
Thou ordainest."

394. Always ponder within yourself in
this wise: "All these family concerns are
not mine; they are God's, and I am His
servant. I have come here to obey His
commands." When this idea becomes
firm, there remains nothing which a man
may call his own.

395. As a wet-nurse in a rich family
brings up the child of her master, loving
the baby as if it were her own, but knows
well that she has no claim upon it; so
think ye also that you are but trustees
and guardians of your children whose real
father is the Lord God in Heaven.

396. Two are the occasions when the
Lord smiles. First, when brothers re-

move the chains which partition off the family property, saying, "This is mine and that is thine"; and secondly, when the physician of a dying patient declares, "I shall make him live."

Caste distinctions. 397. *Q.* Is it proper to keep the Brahmanical thread?

A. When the knowledge of Self is gained, all fetters fall off of themselves. Then there is no distinction between a Brâhmin and a Sudra, a high caste or a low caste. In that state the sacred-thread-sign of caste falls away of itself. But so long as a man has the consciousness of distinction and difference, he should not forcibly throw it off.

398. When a fruit becomes ripe and falls of itself, it tastes very sweet; but when an unripe fruit is plucked and artificially ripened, it does not taste so sweet and becomes shrivelled up. So when a man has realized Brahman in everything, then, and not till then, can he have no distinction of caste. But so long as this exalted state of Divine Wisdom is not reached, none can escape the recognition

142

Sri Ramakrishna.

of superiority and inferiority in others,
and as such one must have to observe
caste distinctions.

399. Once a student questioned Bhagavân Srî Râmakrishna—"As the same
Hari dwells in every being, what harm is
there in taking food out of any man's
hands?" In reply the Bhagavân asked
him whether he was a Brâhmin. When
the student said "Yes," the Bhagavân
said, "That is why you put me the question. Suppose you light a match and
heap over it a lot of well-dried wood, what
will become of the fire?" The student
answered, "The fire will get extinguished,
being choked by the wood." Again the
Bhagavân said, "Suppose a wild fire is
blazing and you throw in it a lot of green
banana trees, what will become of them?"
The student replied, "They will be reduced to ashes in a moment." "Similarly,
said the Bhagavân, "if the spirituality
in you is very weak, you have to fear its
getting extinguished by taking food indiscriminately out of everyone's hands.
If it is very strong, any food that goes
within will not affect you."

400. When a wound is perfectly healed the slough falls off of itself; but if the slough be taken off earlier, it bleeds. Sim ilarly, when the perfection of knowledge is reached by a man, the distinctions o: caste fall off from him, but it is wrong for the ignorant to break such distinctions.

401. When a storm blows it is impos· sible then to distinguish between a pippa: (Asvattha) tree and a banyan (Vata) tree; so when the storm of true knowledge (the knowledge of one universal existence) blows within a man, there can be no dis· tinction of caste.

402. The spiritually-minded belong tc a caste of their own irrespective of all social conventions.

403. When a man is on the plains he sees the lowly grass and the mighty pine tree and says, "How big is the tree and how small is the grass!" But when he ascends the mountain and looks from its high peak on the plain below, the mighty pine tree and the lowly grass blend into one indistinguishable mass of green ver-

Sri Ramakrishna.

dure. So in the sight of the worldly there
are differences of rank and position—one
is a king, another is a cobbler, one a
father, another a son, and so on—but
when the sight Divine is opened, all appear
as equal and one, and there remains no
distinction of good and bad, high and
low.

404. True knowledge leads to unity, **Unity in diversity.**
and ignorance to diversity.

405. When I look upon chaste women
of respectable families, I see in them the
Mother Divine arrayed in the garb of a
chaste lady; and again, when I look upon
the public women of the city, sitting in
their verandas, arrayed in the garb of
immorality and shamelessness, I see in
them also the Mother Divine sporting in
a different way.

406. Man is like a pillow-case. The
color of the one may be red, that of another blue, that of a third black, but all
contain the same cotton. So it is with
man,—one is beautiful, another is black,
a third holy, a fourth wicked, but the
Divine One dwells within them all.

The Sayings of

407. Every being is Nârâyana (Nârâyana is the same as Brahman). Man or
animal, sage or knave, nay, the whole
universe is Nârâyana, the Supreme Spirit.

408. Says God, "I am the snake that
biteth and the charmer that healeth; I
am the judge that condemneth and the
executioner that whippeth."

409. God tells the thief to go and steal,
and at the same time warns the house-
holder against the thief.

410. A jar kept in water is full of water
inside and outside. Thus the soul immersed in God sees the all-pervading
Spirit within and without.

How to conquer human weakness. 411. *Q.* How may we conquer the old
Adam in us?
A. When the fruit grows out of the
flower, the petals drop off of themselves.
So, when the divinity in thee increases,
the weaknesses of thy human nature will
all vanish of their own accord.

412. Humanity must die before divinity manifests itself. But this divinity

Sri Ramakrishna.

must, in turn, die before the higher manifestation of the Blissful Mother takes
place. It is on the bosom of dead divinity
(Shiva) that the Blissful Mother dances
Her dance celestial.

413. If you fill an earthen vessel with **Love of** water and set it apart upon a shelf, the **God.** water in it will dry up in a few days; but if you place the same vessel immersed in water, it will remain filled as long as it is kept there. Even so is the case of your love for the Lord God. Fill and enrich your bosom with the love of God for a time and then employ yourself in other affairs, forgetting Him all the while, and then you are sure to find within a short time that your heart has become poor and vacant and devoid of that precious love. But if you keep your heart immersed always in the ocean of Divine love, your heart is sure to remain ever full to over-flowing with the water of the love Divine.

414. Dear friend, the more I live, the more I learn every day of the mysteries of love and devotion.

The Sayings of

415. *Q.* How should one love God?

A. As the true and chaste wife loves her husband and the niggardly miser loves his hoarded wealth, so the devotee must love the Lord with all his heart and soul.

416. *Q.* Can Divine Love be acquired by reading books?

A. The Hindu almanacs contain predictions of the annual rainfall, mentioning how many inches of rain will fall throughout the country. But if we squeeze the book so full of rain predictions, not even a drop of water can be got out of it. So, also, many good sayings are to be found in holy books, but merely reading them will not make one spiritual. One must practise the virtues taught therein to acquire the love of God.

417. God, His scripture (the Bhâgavata), and His devotee are all to be regarded as one, that is, in one and the same light.

418. *Q.* How does a true lover see God?

A. He sees Him as His nearest and dearest relative, just as the shepherd

Sri Ramakrishna.

women of Brindâvan (Gopi) saw in Srî
Krishna not the Lord of the Universe
(Jagannâtha) but their own beloved
Gopinath (Lord of the Gopi).

419. *Q.* Why does the God-lover find The God-lover.
such ecstatic pleasure in addressing the
Deity as Mother?

A. Because the child is more free with
its mother, and consequently she is
dearer to the child than any one else.

420. A logician once asked Srî Râmakrishna, "What are knowledge, knower,
and the object known?" To which he
replied, "Good man, I do not know all
these niceties of scholastic learning. I
know only my Mother Divine, and that I
am Her son."

421. *Q.* Why does the God-lover renounce everything for Him?

A. The moth, after seeing the light, never
returns to darkness; the ant dies in the
sugar-heap, but never retreats therefrom;
similarly the God-lover gladly sacrifices
his life for the attainment of Divine bliss
and cares for nothing else.

149

422. Some get tipsy with even a small glass of wine, others require two or three bottles to make them intoxicated. But both get equal and full pleasure of intoxication. Similarly, some devotees become full of ecstasy even by a glimpse of the Divine glory, while others get intoxicated with the celestial bliss by coming in direct contact with the Lord of the Universe. But both are equally fortunate and blissful.

423. A true devotee who has drunk deep of Divine Love is like a veritable drunkard and as such cannot always observe the rules of propriety.

424. The more you scratch the ringworm, the greater grows the itching, and the more pleasure do you find in the scratching. Similarly, the devotees once beginning to sing His praises, never get tired of it, but continue for hours and hours together.

Fellowship among true devotees.

425. *Q.* Why does not the God-lover like to live in solitude?

A. The hemp-smoker finds no pleasure in smoking without company. The

pious man like the hemp-smoker finds no
pleasure in singing the sacred name and
praises of the Almighty alone.

426. A woman naturally feels shy to
relate to all the conversation she daily
holds with her husband. She never tells
it to any one, nor feels inclined to do so;
and if it gets divulged by any means she
feels annoyed. But she herself would
relate it without reserve to her intimate
companion, nay, she would feel impa-
tient to tell it to her and find pleasure in
so doing. Similarly, a devotee of God
does not like to relate to any one but a
true Bhakta (devotee) the ecstatic joys
which he experiences in his Divine communion; nay, sometimes he becomes im-
patient of relating his experiences to him
and feels happy to do so.

427. If a strange animal enters a herd
of cows, it is soon driven off by the com-
bined attacks of the whole herd. But
let only a cow enter, all the other cows
will make friends with her by mutual
licking of bodies. Thus, when a devotee
meets with another devotee, both ex-

perience great happiness and feel loath to separate; but when a scoffer enters the circle, they carefully avoid him.

A true devotee's love inexhaustible. 428. *Q.* Why is there no end to the spiritual thoughts and devotional feelings of a devotee?

A. When grains are measured out to the purchaser in the granary of a rich merchant, the measurer does not leave his seat but goes on measuring unceasingly while the attendant women incessantly supply him with basketfuls of grain from the main store; a small grocer, on the other hand, has neither such attendants nor is his store inexhaustible. Similarly, God Himself constantly inspires the new thoughts and the wise sentiments that arise in the heart of his true devotee (Bhakta); whereas the book-learned who draw their inspiration from books are like the petty grocers who soon find their stock exhausted.

429. There are three kinds of love,—unselfish (Samârthâ), mutual (Sâman jasâ), and selfish (Sadhârni). The unselfish love is of the highest kind. The lover

Sri Ramakrishna.

only minds the welfare of the beloved and does not care for his own sufferings. In mutual love the lover not only wants the happiness of his beloved but has an eye towards his own happiness also. It is middling. The selfish love is the lowest. It only looks towards its own happiness, no matter whether the beloved suffers weal or woe.

430. The flint may remain for myriads of years under water, still it does not lose its inner fire. Strike it with steel whenever you like, and out flashes the glowing spark. So is the true devotee firm in his faith. Though he may remain surrounded by all the impurities of the world, he never loses his faith and love. He becomes entranced as soon as he hears the name of the Almighty.

431. A man who finds all the hairs of his body standing on end at the bare mention of *Sri Hari's* name, through sheer ecstasy, and who sheds tears of love on hearing the name of God, he has reached his last birth.

Name of Hari and devotional practices.

432. Hari (from *hri*, to steal) means "He who steals our hearts," and Haribala means "Hari is our strength."

433. Satan never enters the house wherein are always sung the praises of *Hari*.

Prayers and penances. 434. Totâpuri used to say, "If the brass pot be not rubbed daily, it will get rusty. So if a man does not meditate on the Deity daily, his heart will become impure." To him the Bhagavân replied, "Yes, but if the vessel be of gold, it does not require daily cleaning. The man who has reached God, no more requires prayers and penances."

435. *Q.* Is there really any efficacy in prayers?

A. Yes, when mind and speech unite in earnestly asking for a thing, that prayer is answered. The prayers of that man are of no avail who sayeth with his mouth, "These are all Thine, O Lord!" but who at the same time thinketh in his heart all of them to be his.

Sri Ramakrishna.

436. Pray to the Divine Mother in this wise: Give me, O Mother! love that knows no incontinence and faith adamantine that cannot be shaken.

437. He who has faith possesseth all, **Faith.** and he who lacks in faith verily lacks in all.

438. If thou hast faith thou shalt attain to that for which thou longest.

439. Boil your sugar well in a living and active fire. As long as there is earth and impurity in it, the sweet infusion will smoke and simmer. But when all impurity is cast out, there is neither smoke nor sound, but the delicious crystalline fluid heaves itself in its unmixed worth, and whether liquid or solid is the delight of men and gods. Such is the character of the man of faith.

440. A stone may remain for myriads of years in water and the water will never penetrate it. But clay is soon softened and wetted through and through by contact with water. So the strong heart of

the faithful does not despair in the midst
of trials and persecutions, but the man of
weak faith is easily shaken even by the
most trifling cause.

441. The locomotive engine easily drags
along a train of heavily-laden carriages.
So the loving children of God, firm in
their faith and devotion to Him, feel no
trouble in passing through all the worries
and anxieties of life, and leading men along
with them to God.

442. The waters of a swiftly-flowing
current in some places move round and
round in eddies and whirlpools; but
quickly passing these, they resume their
straight and swift course. So the heart
of the pious sometimes falls into the whirlpools of despondency, grief and unbe-
lief; but it is only a momentary aberra-
tion. It does not last long.

443. The anvil of a blacksmith remains
immovable under the countless strokes
of hammers. Even so man should endure
with infinite patience all trials and persecutions that may come upon him.

Sri Ramakrishna.

444. The iron must be heated several
times and hammered a hundred times
before it becomes good steel. Then only
it becomes fit to be made into a sharp
sword and can be bent in any way you
like. So man must be heated several
times in the furnace of tribulations and
hammered with the persecutions of the
world before he becomes pure and humble.

445. If thou wishest to thread the needle, make the thread pointed and remove
all extraneous fibres. Then the thread
will easily enter into the eye of the needle,
So if thou wishest to concentrate thy
heart on God, be meek, humble, and poor
in spirit, and remove all the filaments
of desire.

446. The tree laden with fruit always
bends low. So if thou wishest to be great,
be lowly and meek.

447. The rain-water never stands on
high ground but runs down to the lowest
level; even so the mercy of God runs into
the hearts of the lowly, but drains off
from the hearts of the vain and proud.

448. The scale that is heavy bends down, but the lighter scale of the balance rises up. So the man of merit and ability is always humble and meek, but the fool is always puffed up with vanity.

Vanity. 449. Vanity is like a heap of rubbish or ashes on which the water, as soon as it falls, dries away. Prayers and contemplations produce no effect on the heart puffed up with vanity.

450. Be as devoid of vanity as the castaway leaf before the high wind.

451. The vanities of all others may gradually die out, but the vanity of a saint as regards his sainthood is hard indeed to wear away.

452. A man after fourteen years' penance in a solitary forest obtained at last the power of walking on water. Overjoyed at this, he went to his Guru and said, "Master, master, I have acquired the power of walking on water." The master rebukingly replied, "Fie, O child! is this the result of thy fourteen years'

Sri Ramakrishna.

labors? Verily thou hast obtained only that which is worth a penny; for what thou hast accomplished after fourteen years' arduous labor ordinary men do by paying a penny to the boatman."

453. A youthful disciple of the Bhagavân once acquired the power of reading the heart of another. Overjoyed at this, he related this experience to his master, and the Bhagavân rebuked him by saying, "Shame on thee, child! Do not waste thy energies on these petty things."

454. A certain pious man used to count **Divine** the beads of a rosary constantly, silently **Grace.** uttering the name of the Deity. To him the Bhagavân said, "Why dost thou stick to one place? Go forward." The pious man replied, "It cannot be done without His grace." The Bhagavân said, "The breeze of His Grace is blowing night and day over thy head; unfurl the sails of thy boat (mind), if thou wantest to make rapid progress through the ocean of life."

455. The wind of God's grace is incessantly blowing. Lazy sailors on this

sea of life do not take advantage of it. But the active and the able always keep their minds unfurled to catch the friendly breeze, and thus reach their destination very soon.

456. In this Iron Age three days are enough to make a man perfect.

457. As long as there is no breeze blowing, we fan ourselves to alleviate heat; but when the breeze blows for all men, rich and poor, we give up fanning. We should persevere ourselves to reach our final goal as long as there is no help from above; but when fortunately that help comes to any, let him stop laboring and persevering, otherwise not.

458. Fans should be discarded when the wind blows. Prayers and penances should be discarded when the grace of God descends.

Persever-ance. 459. The hereditary agriculturist does not leave off tilling the soil though it may not rain for twelve consecutive years; while a merchant, who has but lately

Sri Ramakrishna.

taken himself to the plough, is discouraged by one season of drought. The true believer is never discouraged if even with his life-long devotion he fails to see God.

460. Many times must you sink and struggle in water before you learn to swim. So none can enjoy at once the felicity of swimming calmly on the ocean of Divine Bliss until he has made himself fit for it by wearisome struggles and trials.

461. There is little chance of the ship unning amiss so long as its compass points towards the true North. So if the mind of man—the compass needle of the ship of life—is turned always towards the Parabrahman (Absolute Spirit) without oscillation, it will steer clear of every danger.

462. How sweet is the simplicity of a **Become** child! He prefers a doll to all the riches **as a child.** and the wealth of the world. So is the faithful devotee. No one else can throw aside all wealth and all honor to take God only.

161

The Sayings of

463. So long as one does not become simple like a child one does not get Divine illumination. Forget all the worldly knowledge that thou hast acquired and become as ignorant as a child, and then wilt thou get the Divine wisdom.

464. Lunatics, drunkards and children sometimes give out the truth unconsciously, as if inspired by heaven.

Truthfulness. 465. Eternal Truth shall not be realized by one who is not truthful.

Resignation to the will of God. 466. *Q.* What are you to do when you are placed in this world?
A. Give up everything to Him, resign yourself to Him and there will be no more trouble for you. Then you will come to know that everything is done by His will.

467. There is no path safer and smoother than that of *Ba-kalamâ.* *Bakalamâ* means resigning the self to the will of the Almighty, to have no consciousness that anything is "mine."

Sri Ramakrishna.

468. To live in the world or to leave it depends upon the will of God. Therefore work, leaving everything to Him. What else can you do?

469. The value of the figure one (1) may be raised by adding zeroes to it, but if the figure *one* be omitted, the zeroes of themselves have no value. Similarly, so long as the Jiva (individual soul) clings to the Supreme One, it has value—otherwise all of its efforts and works are in vain.

470. *Q*. What is the nature of absolute reliance?

A. It is that happy state of comfort felt by a fatigued worker when, reclining on a pillow, he smokes at leisure after a hard day's toil; it is a cessation of all anxieties and worries.

471. As dry leaves are blown about here and there by the wind and have no choice of their own and make no exertion; so those who depend upon God move in harmony with His will, and can have no will and put forth no effort of their own.

163

472. A shallow pool of water in an open field will soon be dried up though no one may lessen the quantity of water by using it. So a sinner is sometimes purified by simply resigning himself totally and absolutely to the mercy and the grace of God.

473. There are some fish which have many sets of bones, and others have one, but the eater cleans all the bones and eats the fish; so some men have many sins and others have few, but the grace of God purifies them all in time.

474. The young of a monkey clasps and clings to its mother. The young kitten cannot clasp its mother but mews piteously wherever it is placed by her. If the young monkey lets go its hold on its mother, it falls down and gets hurt. This is because it depends upon its own strength; but the kitten runs no such risk, as the mother herself carries it about from place to place. Such is the difference between self-reliance and entire resignation to the will of God.

Thought of Divine Mother. 475. When unavoidably entering into places where there may be temptation,

164

Sri Ramakrishna.

carry always with thee the thought of thy Divine Mother. She will protect thee from the many evils that may be lurking even in thy heart. The presence of thy mother will shame thee away from evil deeds and evil thoughts.

476. Woman and wealth have drowned the whole world in sin. Woman is disarmed when you view her as the manifestation of the Divine Mother.

477. *Q.* Where does the strength of an aspirant lie?

A. He is a child of God, and tears are his greatest strength. As a mother gives her consent to fulfil the desire of her importunately weeping child, so God vouchsafes to His weeping son whatever he is crying for.

Strength of an aspirant.

478. The tears of repentance and the tears of happiness flow from two different corners of the eye. The tears of repentance flow from the side near the nose, and the tears of happiness from the other extremity.

Continual devotion. 479. *Q.* Sometimes peace reigns in the heart, but why does it not always last long?

A. The fire made by the burning of the bamboo is soon extinguished unless kept alive by constant blowing. Continual devotion is necessary to keep alive the fire of spirituality.

480. *Q.* How can I perform devotion when I must always think of my daily bread?

A. He for whom thou workest will supply thy necessities. God hath made provision for thy support before He sent thee here.

481. To kill another swords and shields are needed, whilst to kill one's own self even a pin will do; so to teach others one must study many scriptures and sciences, whilst to acquire self-illumination firm faith in a single motto will suffice.

Single-mindedness. 482. As the village maidens in India carry four or five pots of water placed one over the other upon their heads, talking all the while with one another about their

Sri Ramakrishna.

joys and sorrows, and yet do not allow a
drop of water to get spilt; so must the
traveller in the path of virtue walk along.
In whatever circumstances he may be
placed, let him always take heed that his
heart does not swerve from the true path.

483. Friend, I learn as long as I live.

484. Chant forth the sweet name of **Mental**
Hari (God), keeping time all the while by **concen-**
clapping your hands, and thus you will **tration.**
acquire mental concentration. If you
clap your hands sitting under a tree, the
birds on the boughs thereof will fly away
in all directions, and when you chant
forth the name of *Hari* and clap your
hands, all evil thoughts will fly away from
your mind.

485. As a marksman learns to shoot
by first taking aim at large objects, and
the more he acquires the facility, the
greater becomes the ease with which he
can shoot at smaller marks on the target;
so when the mind has been trained to be
fixed on images having form, it becomes
easy for it to be fixed on images having
no form.

The Sayings of

486. As a boy begins to learn writing
by drawing big scrawls before he can master the small-hand, so we must acquire the
power of concentration by fixing the mind
first on forms, and when we have attained
success therein, we can easily fix it upon
the formless.

487. The easiest means of concentra-
ting the mind is to contemplate the flame
of a candle. Its inmost blue zone is the
causal body or *kârana-sarira*. By fixing
the mind on it concentration is soon obtained. The luminous zone that envelops
the blue flame represents the *sukshma-
sarira* or the subtle body, and the outer-
most represents the gross body or *sthula-
sarira*.

488. At the beginning a man should
always try to concentrate his mind in a
lonely place, otherwise many things
may distract it. If we keep milk and
water together, they are sure to get
mixed; but if the milk be changed into
butter by churning, the transformed milk
(butter), instead of getting itself mixed
with water, will float upon it. So when

Sri Ramakrishna.

by constant practice a man is able to effect mental concentration, wherever he may be, his mind will always rise above his environments and rest on God.

489. In the course of his meditation **Medita-** a beginner sometimes falls into a kind of **tion.** sleep that goes by the name of Yoganidra. At that time he invariably sees some kind of divine visions.

490. "To him who is perfect in meditation salvation is very near," is an old saying. Do you know when a man becomes perfect in meditation? When, as soon as he sits down to meditate, he becomes surrounded with Divine atmosphere and his soul communes with God.

491. He who at the time of contemplation is entirely unconscious of everything outside—so much so that he would not know if birds were to make nests in his hair—has acquired the perfection of meditation.

492. There are few who can attain **State of** Samâdhi and get rid of *Aham* (I-hood). **Samâdhi.** Generally it does not go. Reason and

discriminate indefinitely, this *Aham* comes back to you again and again. To-day you cut the Pepul tree and to-morrow you see it has sprouted forth.

493. When the state of Samâdhi is attained after a process of severe struggle with one's own lower nature and assiduous application to culture for self-knowledge, the ego with all its train vanishes. But it is so difficult to attain Samâdhi. The ego is so persistent. For this reason alone there is the coming again and again into this world.

494. *Q.* What is the state of one's mind in Samâdhi?

A. It is the state of bliss which is experienced by the live fish which, being kept out of water for some time, is again put into it.

495. There are hills and mountains, dales and valleys under the sea, but they are not visible from the surface. So in the state of Samâdhi, when one floats upon the ocean of Sat-chit-ânanda, all human consciousness lies latent.

Sri Ramakrishna.

496. It is a state of going back and forth. You go back to the Supreme Being and your personality becomes one with His personality. This is Samâdhi. You then retrace your steps. You get back your ego and return to the point whence you started, only to see that your ego i derived from the same Supreme Being, and that God, Man, Nature are faces of the one Reality, so that if you hold fast to one of them you realize them all.

497. Do you know how a man of Sâttvika (pure nature) meditates? He meditates in the dead of night, upon his bed, within the curtain, so that he may not be seen by men.

498. *Q.* Should the devotee adopt any particular costume?

A. The adoption of a suitable costume is good. Dressed in the Sannyâsin's orange robes or carrying the religious mendicant's tambourine and cymbals, a man can never utter light and profane things or sing profane songs. But a man dressed in the smart style of a beau will

Should devotee adopt special costume?

naturally have his heart inclined to think
worldly thoughts and sing love songs.

499. *Q.* What is the good of wearing
the orange-colored dress of an ascetic?
What is there in a dress?

A. The orange dress brings with it pure
associations. The wearing of worn-out
shoes and torn clothes brings thoughts of
humility into the mind; dressing smartly
in pants and coat, with patent leather
shoes on, makes one naturally feel elated
with pride and vanity; by wearing the
black-bordered dhoti one feels impelled
to be lively and sing love songs. The
wearing of the orange garb of the Sannyâsin causes sacred thoughts naturally to
enter the mind. Every kind of dress has
its own associations, although the dress in
itself means nothing very particular.

500. If a man sees a pleader, he naturally thinks of cases and causes; similarly, on seeing a pious devotee the man
remembers his God and the hereafter.

501. As in a pane of glass on which
quicksilver has been laid, one can see his

Sri Ramakrishna.

face reflected, so in the chaste heart of a
totally continent devotee is reflected the
image of the Almighty.

502. Of itself does the bee come to the **The per-**
full-blown flower when its sweet aroma **fect man**
is wafted by the breeze. The ants come
of themselves to the spot where sweets
are placed. No one need invite the bee
or the ant. So when a man becomes pure
and perfect, the sweet influence of his
character is diffused everywhere, and all
who seek after truth are naturally drawn
towards him, and he need not be moving
to and fro in search of an audience to
preach the truth to.

"Mother, I am yantra *(the machine),*
Thou art yantri *(one who works the ma-*
chine); I am the room, Thou art the ten-
ant; I am the sheath, Thou art the sword;
I am the chariot, Thou art the charioteer;
I do just as Thou makest me do; I speak
as Thou makest me speak; I behave as
Thou makest me behave; not 'I,' not 'I,'
but 'Thou.'"

PARABLES.

504. A place was enclosed by means of a high wall. The men outside did not know what sort of place it was. Once four persons determined to find out what was inside by scaling the wall with a ladder. As soon as the first man ascended to the top of the wall, he laughed out, "Ha, Ha, Ha!" and jumped in. The second also, as soon as he ascended, similarly laughed aloud and jumped in, and so did the third. When the fourth and last man got up to the top of the wall, he found stretched beneath him a large and beautiful garden containing pleasant groves and delicious fruits. Though strongly tempted to jump down and enjoy the scene, he resisted the temptation, and coming down the ladder, preached the glad tidings about the beautiful garden to all outsiders. The Brahman is like the

177

walled garden. He who sees It forgets
his own existence and with ecstatic joy
rushes headlong unto It to attain to
Moksha or absolute freedom. Such are
the holy men and liberated saints of the
world. But the saviours of humanity are
those who see God, and being at the same
time anxious to share their happiness of
Divine vision with others, refuse the final
liberation (Moksha), and willingly undergo
the troubles of rebirth in the world in order
to teach and lead struggling humanity
to its ultimate goal.

505. A wood-cutter led a very miserable
life with the small means he could procure
by daily selling the load of wood brough
from a neighboring forest. Once a
Sannyâsin, who was wending his way
through the forest, saw him at work and
advised him to proceed onward into th
interior recesses of the forest, intimating
to him that he would be a gainer thereby
The wood-cutter obeyed the injunctio
and proceeded onward until he came t
a sandalwood tree, and being much
pleased, he took away with him as man
sandal logs as he could carry and sold them

in the market and derived much profit. Then he began to think within himself why the good *Sannyâsin* did not tell him anything about the wood of the sandal trees, but simply advised him to proceed onward into the interior of the forest. So the next day he went on beyond the place of the sandalwood, and at last came upon a copper mine, and he took with him as much copper as he could carry, and, selling it in the market, got much money by it. Next day, without stopping at the copper mine, he proceeded further still, as the Sâdhu had advised him to do, and came upon a silver mine, and took with him as much of it as he could carry and sold it all and got even more money; and so daily proceeding further and further, he got at gold mines and diamond mines and at last became exceedingly rich. Such is also the case with the man who aspires after true Knowledge. If he does not stop in his progress after attaining a few extraordinary and supernatural powers, he at last becomes really rich in the eternal knowledge of Truth.

506. A man began to sink a well, but

when he had dug down a few feet another man came to him and said, "Brother, why are you laboring here in vain? You will not find a water-spring underneath; nothing but dry sand will come out." Believing in his words, he left that place and, selecting another spot, he began to dig. There he met a stranger who assured him saying, "Brother, formerly there was a well here, why are you wasting your energy? If you go a little further south and dig, you will find a very good water-spring." Immediately he followed his advice; but there again another man prevented him from digging. Thus being interrupted again and again at every spot which he had selected, he at last failed to sink the well. Similarly in the spiritual path many people have lost everything by following the directions of irresponsible instructors. Now they follow one master, but, having neither firmness of faith nor strength to resist the temptations, trials and tribulations which come in their way, they abandon him and obey another, and then a third; and so eventually they either become rank atheists or arrive at the con-

Sri Ramakrishna.

clusion that in this life it is impossible
to attain spirituality. He, however, who
wishes to be spiritual must have firm faith
in one master and follow his directions
with implicit obedience and infinite
patience.

507. A man wanted to cross the river.
A sage gave him an amulet and said,
"This will carry thee across." The man,
taking it in his hand began, to walk over
the waters. When he reached the middle
of the river, curiosity entered into his
heart, and he opened the amulet to see
what was in it. Therein he found, written
on a piece of paper, the sacred name of
Râma (Lord). The man at this said
deprecatingly, "Is this the only secret?"
No sooner had he said this than he sank
down. It is faith in the name of the
Lord that works miracles, for faith is life
and doubt is death.

508. Bhagavân Srî Râmachandra had
to bridge the ocean before he could cross
over to Lamkâ (Ceylon). But Hanu-
mân, his faithful monkey-servant, with
one jump crossed the ocean through the

firmness of his faith in Râma. Here the servant achieved more than the master, simply through faith.

509. A disciple, having firm faith in the infinite power of his Guru, walked over a river even by pronouncing his name. The Guru, seeing this, thought within himself, "Well, is there such a power even in my name? Then I must be very great and powerful, no doubt!" The next day he also tried to walk over the river pronouncing "I, I, I," but no sooner had he stepped into the waters than he sank and was drowned. Faith can achieve miracles, while vanity or egoism is the death of man.

510. A milk-maid used to supply milk to a Brâhmin priest living on the other side of the river. Owing to the irregularities of boat service, she could not supply it punctually every day. Once being rebuked for her lateness, the poor woman said, "What can I do? I start early from my house but have to wait a long time at the river bank for the boatman and the

Sri Ramakrishna.

passengers." The priest said, "Woman! they cross the ocean of life by uttering the name of God and canst thou not cross this little river?" The simple-hearted woman became very glad at heart, on finding this easy means of crossing the river. From the next day the milk was supplied early in the morning, and the milk-maid was also happy, as she saved her fare. One day the priest said to the woman, "How is it that you are no longer late now?" She said, "I cross the river by uttering the name of the Lord as you told me to do, and don't stand in need of the boatman." The priest could not believe this and said, "Canst thou show me how thou crossest the river?" The woman took him with her and began to walk over the water. Looking behind, the woman saw his sad plight and said, "How is this, Sir, thou art uttering the name of the Deity with thy mouth, but at the same time with thy hands thou art trying to keep thy clothes untouched by water? Thou dost not fully rely on the Deity." Entire resignation and absolute faith in God are at the root of all miraculous deeds.

511. A father was once passing by a field having his two sons with him. One he had taken up in his arms and the other was walking along with him holding his father's hand. They saw a kite flying, and this boy, having let go his hold on his father's hand, began to clap with joy, crying, "See, papa! there is a kite!" But as he had let go the hold of his father's hand he stumbled and got hurt. But the boy that was carried by the father also clapped his hands with joy, but did not fall as he was held by his father. The former represents self-help in spiritual life while the latter indicates self-surrender.

512. Two men went into a garden. The worldly-wise man no sooner entered the gate than he began to count the number of the mango-trees, how many mangoes each tree bore, and what might be the approximate price of the orchard. His companion went to the owner, made his acquaintance, and quietly going under a mango-tree, began to pluck the fruit and eat it with the owner's consent. Now who is the wiser of the two? Eat man-

Sri Ramakrishna.

goes, it will satisfy your hunger. What is the good of counting the leaves and of vain calculations? The proud man of intellect is vainly busy in finding out the "why and wherefore" of creation, while the humble man of wisdom makes acquaintance with the creator and enjoys Supreme Bliss in this world.

513. Once the Bhagavân, addressing one of his favorite disciples, said: "When syrup is kept in a large basin flies come from all sides and sit upon it. Some drink the sweet juice sitting on the brim of the vessel, while others fall into it and enjoy rolling and plunging into it. Similarly, will you taste the Divine nectar of Sachchidânanda (absolute existence, intelligence and bliss) leisurely from the brim and then flee from it, or will you enjoy the pleasure of tasting it and of plunging yourself at once into it?" The disciple replied: "I like to drink from the brim and fly away and live, but not to roll in the juice and die." At this the Master said: "You fool! He who plunges himself into the ocean of nectar never dies but becomes immortal."

514. Râmachandra, after being enlightened by the precepts of his Guru, determined to renounce the world. Dasaratha, his father, sent the sage Vasistha to instruct him. Vasistha saw that intense Vairâgyam (non-attachment) had come upon Râma. He said, "Râma, first reason with me and then leave the world. I ask you, is the world separate from God? If it be so, you are at liberty to forsake it." Pondering over these words Râma saw that it was God who manifested Himself as the Jiva (individual ego) and the world. In His Being everything existed. So Râma remained silent.

515. When it was argued that a familyman (Grihastha) may remain in the family, but may have no concern with it, and consequently may remain uncontaminated by the world, an illustration was cited to refute such an argument, which is as follows:

A poor Brâhmin once came to one of those family-men who are unconcerned with family affairs, to beg some money. When the beggar asked of him some money, he replied, "Sir, I never touch money.

Sri Ramakrishna.

Why are you wasting your time in begging of me?" The Brâhmin, however, would not go away. Tired with his importunate entreaties, the man at last resolved in his mind to give him a rupee, and told him, "Well, sir, come to-morrow, I shall see what I can do for you." Then going in, this typical family-man told his wife, who was the manager of his affairs, he being unconcerned, "Look here, dear, a poor Brâhmin is in great difficulty, and wants something of me. I have made up my mind to give him a rupee. What is' your opinion about it?" "Aha! what a generous fellow you are!" she replied at the name of a rupee. "Rupees are not like leaves and stones, to be thrown away without any thought." "Well, dear," replied the husband in an apologizing tone, "The man is very poor and we should not give him less than a rupee." "No!" replied the wife, "I cannot spare that much; here is a two-anna bit and you can give him that if you like." The man of course had no other alternative, being himself unconcerned in all such worldly matters, and he took what his wife gave him. Next day the beggar

came and received only a two-anna bit.
Such uncontaminated family-men are
really hen-pecked persons who are solely
guided by their wives, and as such are
very poor specimens of humanity.

516. Once a God-intoxicated Sâdhu
(saint) came to the Kâli-temple of Râni
Rashmoni where the Bhagavân lived.
One day this saint did not get any food,
and, though feeling hungry, he did not
ask anybody for it; but seeing a dog eat-
·ing the remnants of a feast thrown away
in a corner on used leaf-dishes, he went
there, and embracing the dog said,
"Brother, how is it that thou eatest without giving me a share?" So saying, he
began to eat along with the dog. Having finished his meal in this strange company, the sage entered the temple of the
mother Kâli and prayed with such earnestness of devotion as made the temple almost
shake. When having finished his prayer,
he was going away, the Bhagavân told
his cousin, Hridoy Mukerjee, "Go and
follow this man and tell me what he says."
Hridoy followed him to some distance,
when the sage turning round said, "Why

Sri Ramakrishna.

followest thou me?" Hridoy replied,
"Sir! Give me some advice." The sage
replied, "When the water of the dirty
ditch and the yonder glorious Ganges will
appear one in thy sight, and the sound of
this flageolet and the noise of that crowd
will have no distinction to thy ear, then
thou shalt reach the Divine wisdom."

When Hridoy returned and told the
Bhagavân, he said, "That man reached
the higher state of ecstasy which is the
result of Divine wisdom."

The *Sâdhus* roam about like children
or like mad-men, and in various other
disguises.

517. Once a holy man (*Sâdhu*) while
passing through a crowded street acci-
dentally trod upon the toe of a wicked
person. The wicked man, furious with
rage, beat the saint mercilessly till he fell
on the ground in a state of unconscious-
ness. His disciples took great pains and
adopted various measures to bring him
back to consciousness, and when they saw
that he was coming round a little, one of
them asked, "Sir, do you recognize who
is now serving you?" The Sâdhu re-

plied, "He who beat me." A true saint finds no distinction between friend and foe.

518. The Avadhûta (a great Yogi) saw a bridal procession passing through a meadow with the beating of drums and the blowing of trumpets and with great pomp. Hard by the road through which the procession was passing he saw a hunter deeply absorbed in aiming at a bird, and perfectly inattentive to the noise and pomp of the procession, casting not even a passing look at it. The Avadhûta, saluting the hunter, said, "Sir, thou art my Guru. When I sit in meditation, let my mind be concentrated upon the object of meditation as thine has been on the bird."

519. An angler was fishing in a pond. The Avadhûta (a great Yogi) approaching him asked, "Brother, which way leads to such and such a place?" The float of the rod at that time was indicating that the fish was nibbling the bait; so the man did not give any reply but was all attention to his fishing-rod. When the fish was

Sri Ramakrishna.

caught, he turned round and said, "What is it you have been saying, sir?" The Avadhûta saluted him and said, "Sir, thou art my Guru. When I sit in the contemplation of the *Paramâtman* (the Supreme Spirit), let me follow thy example and before finishing my devotions let me not attend to anything else."

520. A heron was slowly walking to catch a fish. Behind, there was a hunter aiming an arrow at it, but the bird was totally unmindful of this fact. The Avadhûta (a great Yogi) saluting the heron said: "When I sit in meditation, let me follow thy example and never turn back to see who is behind me."

521. A kite with a fish in its beak was followed by a host of crows and other kites, which were screeching and pecking at it and were trying to snatch the fish away. In whatever direction it went the crowd of kites and crows followed it screeching and cawing. Getting tired of this annoyance the kite let go the fish, when it was instantly caught by another kite and at once the crowd of kites and

crows transferred their kind attentions to the new owner of the fish. The first kite was left unmolested and sat calmly on the branch of a tree. Seeing this quiet and tranquil state of the bird, the Avadhûta (a great Yogi) saluting him, said: "Thou art my Guru, OKite, for thou hast taught me that so long as man does not throw off the burden of the worldly desires he carries, he cannot at all be undisturbed and at peace with himself."

522. It is said that when a Tantrika tries to invoke the Deity through the medium of the spirit of the dead, he sits over a fresh human corpse and keeps near him food and wine. During the invocation, if at any time the corpse is vivified (though temporarily) and opens its mouth, the intrepid invoker must pour the wine and the food into its gaping mouth at the time to appease the elemental that has, for the time being, taken possession of the dead body. If he does not do so, the invocation is interrupted by this elemental and the higher spirit does not descend. So, dwelling in the bosom of the carcase of the world, if thou

Sri Ramakrishna.

wantest to attain beatitude, thou must first provide thyself beforehand with everything necessary to pacify the clamor of all worldly demands on thee, otherwise thy devotions will be broken and interrupted by worldly cares and anxieties.

523. The alligator loves to swim on the surface of the water, but as soon as he rises up he is made a mark of by the hunters. Necessarily he is obliged to remain under water and cannot rise to the surface. Still, whenever he finds an opportunity, he rises up with a deep whizzing noise and swims happily on the wide watery expanse. O man, entangled in the meshes of the world! Thou too art anxious to swim on the surface of the ocean of Bliss, but art prevented from doing so by the importunate demands of thy family. But be of good cheer, and whenever thou findest any leisure call intensely upon thy God, pray to him earnestly, and tell Him all thy sorrows. In His proper time He will surely emancipate thee and enable thee to swim merrily on the surface of the ocean of Bliss.

524. The maid-servant says with reference to her master's house, "This is our house." All the while she knows that the house is not her own, and that her own house is far away in a distant village of Burdwan or Nuddea. Her thoughts are all sent forth to her village home. Again, referring to her master's child in her arms, she says, "My Hari (that being the name of the child) has grown very naughty," or, "My Hari likes to eat this or that," and so on. But all the while she knows for certain that Hari is not her own. I tell those who come to me to lead a life unattached like this maid-servant. I tell them to live unattached to this world—to be in the world, but not of the world—and at the same time to have their mind directed to God, the heavenly home from whence all come. I tell them to pray for Bhakti.

525. A learned Brâhmin once went to a wise king and said: "Hear, O king! I am well versed in the Holy Scriptures. I intend to teach thee the holy book of Bhâgavata." The king, who was the wiser of the two, well knew that a man

Sri Ramakrishna.

who had really studied the Bhâgavata
would seek more to know his own Self
than honor and wealth in a king's court.
He replied: "I see, O Brâhmin, that you
yourself have not mastered that book
thoroughly. I promise to make you my
tutor, but go first and learn the scripture well." The Brâhmin went his way
thinking within himself: "How foolish
the king is to say I have not mastered
the Bhâgavata well, when I have been
reading the book over and over for all
these years." However, he went over
the book carefully once more and appeared before the king. The king told
him the same thing again and sent him
away. The Brâhmin was sore vexed,
but thought that there must be some
meaning for this behavior of the king.
He went home, shut himself up in his
closet and applied himself more than ever
to the study of the book. By and by the
hidden meanings began to flash before his
intellect; the vanity of running after the
bubbles, riches and honor, kings and
courts, wealth and fame, all vanished
before his unclouded vision. From that
day forward he gave himself up entirely

to attain perfection by the worship of
God and never returned to the king.
A few years after, the king thought of
the Brâhmin and went to his house to
see what he was about. Seeing the
Brâhmin all radiant with the divine
light and love, he fell upon his knees
and said, "I see that thou hast now ar-
rived at the true meaning of the Scriptures. I am ready to be thy disciple
if thou wilt duly condescend to make
me one."

526. A Jnâni (knower of God) and a
Premika (lover of God) were once passing through a forest. On the way they
saw a tiger at a distance. The Jnâni
said, "There is no reason why we should
flee; the Almighty God will certainly
protect us." At this the Premika said,
"No, brother, come, let us run away.
Why should we trouble the Lord for what
can be accomplished by our own exertions?"

527. In the month of June a young goat
was playing near his mother, when with a

Sri Ramakrishna.

merry frisk he told her that he meant to
make a feast of Râs-flowers, a species of
flowers budding abundantly during the
time of the Râslilâ festival. "Well, my
darling." replied the dam, "it is not such
an easy thing as you seem to think. You
will have to pass through many crises
before you can hope to feast on Râs-
flowers. The interval between the coming September and October is not very
auspicious to you; for some one may take
you for a sacrifice to the Goddess Durgâ,
then you will have to get through the time
of Kâli-pujâ, and if you are fortunate
enough to escape through that period,
there comes the Jagaddhâtripûjâ, when
almost all the surviving male members
of our tribe are destroyed. If your good
luck leads you safe and sound through all
these crises then you can hope to make
a feast of Râs-flowers in the beginning
of November." Like the dam in the
fable, we should not hastily approve of
all the aspirations which our youthful
hopes may entertain by remembering
the manifold crises which we shall have
to pass through in the course of our
lives.

528. Four blind men went to see an elephant. One touched the leg of the elephant and said, "The elephant is like a pillar." The second touched the trunk and said, "The elephant is like a thick club." The third touched the belly and said, "The elephant is like a big jar." The fourth touched the ears and said: "The elephant is like a big winnowing basket." Thus they began to dispute among themselves as to the figure of the elephant. A passerby seeing them thus quarrelling said, "What is it that you are disputing about?" They told him everything and asked him to arbitrate. The man said, "None of you has seen the elephant. The elephant is not like a pillar, its legs are like pillars. It is not like a big water-vessel, its belly is like a big water-vessel. It is not like a winnowing basket, its ears are like winnowing baskets. It is not like a stout club, but its proboscis is like that. The elephant is the combination of all these." In the same manner those quarrel who have seen only one aspect of the Deity.

529. Be not like Ghantâ Karna in thy

Sri Ramakrishna.

bigotry. There was a man who worshipped Shiva but hated all other Deities. One day Shiva appeared to him and said, "I shall never be pleased with thee so long as thou hatest the other gods." But the man was inexorable. After a few days Shiva again appeared to him and said, "I shall never be pleased with thee so long as thou hatest." The man kept silent. After a few days Shiva again appeared to him. This time he appeared as Hari-har, namely, one side of his body was that of Shiva, and the other side that of Vishnu. The man was half pleased and half displeased. He laid his offerings on the side representing Shiva, and did not offer anything to the side representing Vishnu. Then Shiva said, "Thy bigotry is unconquerable. I, by assuming this dual aspect, tried to convince thee that all gods and goddesses are but various aspects of the one Absolute Brahman."

530. Once a dispute arose in the court of the Mahârâjah of Burdwan among the learned men there as to who was the greater Deity, Shiva or Vishnu. Some gave preference to Shiva, others to Vishnu.

When the dispute grew hot a wise pandit remarked, addressing the Râjâ, "Sire, I have neither met Shiva nor seen Vishnu; how can I say who is the greater of the two?" At this the dispute stopped, for none of the disputants really had seen the Deity. Similarly none should compare one Deity with another. When a man has really seen a Deity, he comes to know that all the Deities are manifestations of one and the same Brahman.

531. Many roads lead to Calcutta. A certain man started from his home in a distant village towards the metropolis. He asked a man on the road, "What road must I take to reach Calcutta soon?" The man said, "Follow this road." Proceeding some distance, he met another man and asked him, "Is this the shortest road to Calcutta?" The man replied, "O, no You must retrace your footsteps and take the road to your left." The man did so Going in that new road for some distance he met a third man, who pointed him out another road to Calcutta. Thus the trav-eller made no progress, but spent the day in changing one road for another. As he

wanted to reach Calcutta, he should have stuck to the road pointed out to him by the first man. Similarly those who want to reach God must follow one, and one only Guide (Guru).

532. A Brâhmin was laying out a garden. He looked after it day and night. One day a cow straying into the garden browsed away a mango sapling which was one of the most carefully watched trees of the Brâhmin. The Brâhmin, seeing the cow destroy his favorite plant, became wild with rage and gave such a sound beating to the animal that she died of the injuries received. The news soon spread like wildfire that the Brâhmin had killed the sacred animal. The Brâhmin was a so-called *Vedântist* and when taxed with the sin, denied it, saying: "No, I have not killed the cow; it is my hand that has done it; and as Indra is the presiding deity of the hand, if any one has incurred the guilt of killing the cow, it is Indra, and not I."

Indra in his heaven heard all this, assumed the shape of an old Brâhmin, came to the owner of the garden, and said, "Sir, whose garden is this?"

Brâhmin—"Mine."

Indra—"It is a beautiful garden. Yo
have got a skillful gardener, for see ho⌐
neatly and artistically he has planted th
trees!"

Brâhmin—"Well, Sir, that is also m⌐
work. The trees were planted under m⌐
personal supervision and direction."

Indra—"Indeed! O, you are ver⌐
clever. But who has laid out this road? I
is very ably planned and neatly executed."

Brâhmin—"All this has been done b⌐
me."

Then Indra with joined hands said
"When all these things are yours and yo⌐
take credit for all the works done in thi⌐
garden, it is hard lines for poor Indra to b⌐
responsible for the killing of the cow."

533. A thief entered the palace of a kin⌐
at the dead of night and overheard the kin⌐
saying to the queen, "I shall give m⌐
daughter to one of those *Sâdhus* (hol⌐
saints) who are dwelling on the banks of th⌐
river." The thief thought within him
self: "Well, here is luck for me. I will g⌐
and sit among the *Sâdhus* to-morrow i⌐
the disguise of a *Sâdhu* and perchance

Sri Ramakrishna.

may succeed in getting the king's daughter." The next day he did so, and when the king's officers came soliciting the *Sâdhus* to marry the king's daughter, none of them consented; at last they came to this thief in the dress of a *Sâdhu* and made the same proposal to him. The thief kept quiet. The officers went back and told the king that there was a young *Sâdhu* who might be influenced to marry the princess, and that there was no other who would consent. The king was obliged to go in person to the *Sâdhu* and intreat him earnestly to honor him by accepting the hand of his daughter. But the heart of the thief was changed by the king going to him. He thought within himself, "I have assumed the dress of the *Sâdhu* and behold the king himself comes to me with entreaties and prayers. Who can say what better things may not be in store for me if I become a real *Sâdhu!*" These thoughts so strongly affected him that instead of marrying under false pretences, he began to mend his ways from that very day and exerted himself to become a true Sâdhu. He did not marry at all and ultimately became one of the most holy saints of his day. The imitation of a good thing sometimes produces genuine results.

When a thief dressed in the garb of a *Sâdhu* could be transformed into a saintly character by associating with the holy ones for so short a time, who can describe the wonderful power of the true saints and of their holy company!

534. A person deeply involved in debts, feigned madness to escape the consequences of his liabilities. Physicians failed to cure the disease; and the more he was treated for his ailment, the greater became his madness. At last a wise physician found out the truth and taking the feigning madman aside, rebuked him, saying: "Sir, what are you doing? Beware, lest in feigning madness, you become really mad. Already I see some genuine signs of insanity in you." This home-thrust advice awoke the man from his folly and he left off acting the part of a madman. By constantly acting a thing one ultimately becomes that thing.

535. The parable of a Brâhmin and his low-caste servant:

Sri Ramakrishna.

As soon as Mâyâ is found out, she flies away. A priest was once going to the village of a disciple. He had no servant with him. On the way, seeing a cobbler, he addressed him saying, "Hallo! good man, wilt thou accompany me as a servant? Thou shalt dine well and wilt be well cared for; come along." The cobbler replied, "Reverend Sir, I am of the lowest caste; how can I represent your servant?" The priest said, "Never mind that. Do not tell anybody what thou art, nor speak to or make acquaintance with any one." The cobbler agreed. At twilight, while the priest was sitting at prayers in the house of his disciple, another Brâhmin came and addressed the priest's servant, "Fellow, go and bring my shoes from there." The servant, true to the words of his master, made no response. The Brâhmin repeated the order a second time, but the servant remained silent. The Brâhmin repeated again and again, but the cobbler moved not an inch. At last getting annoyed, the Brâhmin angrily said, "Hallo, Sirrah! How darest thou not obey a Brâhmin's command! What is thy caste? Art thou a cobbler?" The cobbler, hearing

this. began to tremble with fear, and
piteously looking at the priest, said, "O
venerable Sir! O venerable Sir! I am
found out. I cannot stay here any longer;
let me flee." So saying, he took to his
heels.

536. Haridâsa wearing the mask of a
tiger's head was frightening a young boy.
The mother said to the frightened child,
"Why fearest thou, my dear child? He
is no other than our Hari. He has put on
a paper mask." But the boy still con-
tinued to cry out at the top of his voice.
After a while Hari took the mask off his
face and consoled him by putting it in his
hands; the boy then understood the whole
trick and was no longer frightened by it.
Even such is the case of the worldly that are
deluded and frightened by the inscrutable
power of Mâyâ, under whose mask resides
the ever-Blissful Brâhman. But he who
has gone beyond the veil of Mâyâ is never
disturbed by fear or troubles.

537. Two persons, it is said, began together invoking the Goddess Kâli by the
terrible process called "*Savasâdhana.*" (This

Sri Ramakrishna.

Tantrik invocation is performed in a funeral yard, the invoker sitting on the body of a corpse in a dark night). One invoker was frightened to insanity by the horrors of the earlier portion of the night; the other was favored with the vision of the Divine Mother at the end of the night. Then he asked Her, "Mother! why did the other man become mad?" The Deity answered, "Thou, too, O child! didst become mad many times in thy previous births and now at last thou seest me."

538. A man who was out of employment was constantly bothered by his wife to get some employment. One day when his son was dangerously ill he went out in search of employment. In the meantime his son died and a search was made for the father, but he could not be found anywhere. At last, late in the evening he was seen returning and was severely taken to task for his heartless conduct in leaving the house at a time when his son lay dying. The man replied, "Well, once I dreamt that I had seven sons with whom I passed the time happily. But when I woke up I found that it was all a dream. Well, I never grieved for my

dream of seven sons. Why should I be grieved for this?"

539. Do not give charity indiscriminately; for almsgiving to some persons causes sin, instead of merit. A person had a charitable institution for giving food to every wayfarer who asked for it. A butcher tired of driving a cow to a slaughterhouse, went to the institution, and being invigorated with fresh food and drink, easily drove the cow to the shambles. The sin of killing the cow was divided between the butcher and the author of the institution, in the proportion of four annas and twelve annas.

540. A snake dwelt in a certain place. No one dared to pass by that way; for whoever did so was instantaneously bitten to death. Once a Mahâtman (high-souled one) passed by that road, and the serpent ran after the sage in order to bite him. But when the snake approached the holy man he lost all his ferocity and was overpowered by the gentleness of the Yogin. Seeing the snake, the sage said: "Well, friend thinkest thou to bite me?" The snake

Sri Ramakrishna.

was abashed and made no reply. At this
the sage said: "Hearken, friend; do not
injure anybody in future." The snake
bowed and nodded assent. The sage went
his own way, and the snake entered his
hole, and thenceforward began to live a
life of innocence and purity without even
attempting to harm anyone. In a few
days all the neighborhood began to think
that the snake had lost all his venom and
was no more dangerous, and so everyone
began to tease him. Some pelted him;
others dragged him mercilessly by the tail,
and in this way there was no end to his
troubles. Fortunately the sage again
passed by that way, and seeing the bruised
and battered condition of the good snake,
was very much moved, and inquired the
cause of his distress. At this the snake
replied: "Holy Sir, this is because I do
not injure any one after your advice. But
alas! they are so merciless!" The sage
smilingly said: "My dear friend, I simply
advised you not to bite anyone, but I did
not tell you not to frighten others. Although you should not bite any creature,
still you should keep everyone at a con-
siderable distance by hissing at him."

Similarly, if thou livest in the world,
make thyself feared and respected. Do
not injure any one, but be not at the same
time injured by others.

541. A fisherwoman on her way home
from a distant market was overtaken by a
storm at nightfall, so she was compelled to
take refuge in a florist's house near at hand.
The hospitable florist received her very
kindly and allowed her to spend the night
in a room next to his garden. But the
fragrant atmosphere of the place was too
good for the fisherwoman. She could not
sleep for a long time. At last when she
discovered that the sweet aroma of the
flowers in the garden kept her awake, she
sprinkled water on her empty basket of
fish, placed it close to her nose, and immediately fell into a sound sleep. Such indeed is the power and influence of bad habits
over all those who are addicted to them.
They cannot enjoy the uplifting influence of the spiritual atmosphere.

542. A rich Marawaree (merchant)
asked the Bhagavân, "Lord, I have renounced everything; why then do I not

Sri Ramakrishna.

find God?" To him the Bhagavân replied; "Your mind is like the leather jar of oil from which, though all the oil has been removed, the scent of the oil still remains. So, though your mind has renounced the world, the scent of worldly desires still clings to you."

543. A disciple once asked the Bhagavân how to conquer lust, for, though he passed his life in religious contemplation, yet evil thoughts did arise in his mind now and then. The Bhagavân replied: There was a man who had a pet dog. He would caress him, carry him about on his lap, play with him, and kiss him. A wise man, seeing the folly, told him not to give so much indulgence to his dog. It was an unreasoning brute after all and might bite him one of these days. The owner of the dog took the advice to heart and, throwing away the dog from his lap, resolved never again to fondle and caress him. But the dog could not understand the changed feelings of his master and would run to him frequently to be taken up and caressed. Being beaten several times, the dog at last desisted from troubling his master. Such

is your condition also. The dog of lust that you have nourished so long in your bosom will not easily leave you though you may wish to leave him. However, there is no harm in it; though the dog may come to you to be fondled, do not caress him, but give him a good beating whenever he approaches you, and in course of time you will be freed from his importunities.

544. A husband and wife renounced the world and jointly undertook a pilgrimage to various religious shrines. Once, as they were walking on a road, the husband, being a little ahead of the wife, saw a piece of diamond on the road. Immediately he scratched the ground to hide the diamond, thinking that, if his wife saw it, she might perchance be moved by avarice and thus lose the merit of her renunciation. While he was thus busy, the wife came up and asked him what he was doing. In an apologetic tone he gave her an evasive reply. She noticed the diamond, however, and reading his thoughts, asked him, "Why have you left the world, if you still feel the difference between the diamond and the dust?"

Sri Ramakrishna.

545. A poor Brâhmin had a rich cloth merchant as his disciple. The merchant was one of the most miserly of men. One day the Brâhmin stood in need of a small piece of cloth to serve as a covering for his sacred book. Going to his disciple, he asked for a small piece of cloth.˙ The merchant replied: "I am very sorry, sir; had you told me of this a few hours earlier I would have given you the thing wanted. Unfortunately I have now no small piece of cloth available for your purposes; however, I will keep your wish in mind. Remind me now and then of it, if you please." The Brâhmin went away disappointed. The conversation between the Guru and his worthy disciple was overheard by the wife of the latter from behind a screen. She at once sent a man after the Brâhmin and, calling him inside the house, asked him, "Reverend father, what was it that you were asking from the master of the house?" The Brâhmin related all that had happened. The wife said, "Please go home, sir; you will get the cloth to-morrow morning." When the merchant returned home at night, the wife asked him,"Have you closed the shop?" The merchant said,

The Sayings of

"Yes, what is the matter?" She said, "Go at once and bring two of the best cloths in the shop." He said, "Where is the hurry? I will give you the very best cloths to-morrow morning." The wife said, "No, I must have them just now or not at all." What could the merchant do? It was not the spiritual Guru whom he could send away with vague and indefinite promises, but it was the *curtain Guru*, whose behests must be instantaneously obeyed or there would be no peace for him at home at all. At last the merchant willingly enough went at that late hour of the night, opened the shop, and brought them for her. Early the next morning the good lady of the house sent the cloths to the Guru with this message: "If in future you want anything from us, ask of me and you will get it." Therefore those who pray to the merciful Divine Mother and ask for Her blessings have better chances of having their prayers heard than those who worship God in His sterner Paternal aspect.

546. *Q.* Why do you not lead a family life with your wife?

Sri Ramakrishna.

A. The God Kârtikeya, the leader of the Heavenly army, once happened to scratch a cat with his nail. On going home he saw there was the mark of a scratch on the cheek of his Mother. Seeing this, he asked of her, "Mother, dear, how have you got that ugly scratch on your cheek?" The Goddess Durgâ replied: "Child, this is thy own handiwork—the mark scratched by thy own nail." Kârtikeya asked in wonder, "Mother, how is it? I never remember to have scratched thee!" The Mother replied, "Darling, hast thou forgotten having scratched a cat this morning?" Kârtikeya said, "Yes, I did scratch a cat; but how did your cheek get marked?" The Mother replied, "Dear child, nothing exists in this world but myself. I am all creation. Whomsoever thou hurtest, thou hurtest me." Kârtikeya was greatly surprised at this, and determined never to marry; for whom would he marry? Every woman was mother to him. I am like Kârtikeya. I consider every woman as my Divine Mother.

547. A Brâhmin met a Sannyâsin and they had a long talk on worldly and re-

ligious topics. At last the Sannyâsin addressed the Brâhmin: "Behold, child, there is no depending upon anybody in this world." The Brâhmin would not believe it. How could he believe that those for whom he labored day and night, that is, his own family, were not his friends upon whom he could count for help? So the Brâhmin said: "Sir, when I am troubled with a slight headache, my mother, who is always ready to give up her life in order to save me from danger and to make me comfortable and happy, becomes extremely concerned; that such a mother is not a friend is what I cannot conceive." The Sannyâsin replied: "If such be the case, then of course they are your own. But, to tell you the truth, you are greatly mistaken. Never believe for a moment that your mother, wife, or son will sacrifice her or his life for your sake. You can make a trial of it if you like; go home and feign excruciating pain and groan under it; I will come and show you the fun."

The Brâhmin acted accordingly. Doctors and physicians were called in, but no one could afford relief. The mother of the patient was sighing and sorrowing, the

Sri Ramakrishna.

wife and children were crying. The Sannyâsin turned up at this moment.

"The disease is of a serious nature," said
the Sannyâsin, "and I do not see any chance
of the patient's recovery, unless some one
comes forward to give her or his life for the
sake of the patient." At this all of them
looked aghast. The Sannyâsin, addressing
the old mother of the patient, said: "To
live or to die will be the same thing to you,
if in your old age you lose your son who
earns for himself and for you all. If you can
give your life in exchange for his, I can
save your son. If you, as mother, cannot
make this sacrifice for him, who else in this
world will care to do it?"

The old woman blubbered through her
tears: "Reverend Father, I am ready to
do anything you order for the sake of my
son. But the thing is, my own life—
and what is my life in comparison to that
of my son? The thought—what will become of my little ones after my death—
makes me a coward. Unfortunate that
I am, these little ones are in my way."

While listening to this dialogue between
the Sannyâsin and the mother-in-law, the
wife of the patient wept bitterly and said,

addressing her parents, "For your sake,
dear mother and father, I cannot make the
sacrifice." The Sannyâsin turned to her
and asked her whether she could not sacrifice her life for the sake of her husband
now that his mother fell back. The wife
said: "The wretch that I am! If widow-
hood is to be my lot, be it so. I cannot
make up my mind to entail grief for the
loss of their child upon my father and
mother." In this way every one wrig-
gled out of the difficulty. Then the Sannyâsin addressed the patient and said:
"Look now, no one is ready here to sacrifice his life for you. Do you understand
now what I meant by saying that there
was no depending on anybody here?"
When the Brâhmin saw all this, he aban-
doned his so-called home and followed the
Sannyâsin.

548. He who is fond of fishing and
wishes to be informed if good fishes abound
in a certain pond, quickly goes to those
persons who have fished in it, and eagerly
asks them: "Is it true that there are big
fishes in this pond? If so, what is the
bait to catch them?" Having collected

Sri Ramakrishna.

all this information, he resorts to the pond
with his fishing rod, waits there, throwing
his line, and allures the fish with patience
and dexterity, and at last succeeds in
hooking a large and beautiful dweller of the
deep. So, putting implicit trust in the sayings of holy saints and sages, one must try
to catch and confine God in his bosom with
the bait of devotion and the rod and hook
of mind. With patience one must wait, and
then only can one catch the Divine Fish.

549. A king having committed the mor-
tal crime of killing a Brâhmana, went to the
hermitage of a sage to learn what penance
he must perform in order to be purified.
The sage was absent from home, but his
son was there. The son hearing the case
of the king, said, "Repeat the name of God
(Râma) three times and your sin will be ex-
piated." When the sage came back and
heard the penance prescribed by his son, he
said to him in great wrath, "Sins committed in myriads of births are purged at
once by but once uttering the name of the
Almighty; how weak must be thy faith,
O son, that thou hast ordered that name to
be repeated thrice! For this offence of

thine go and become a Chândâla." And the son became the Guhaka Chândâla of the Râmâyana.

550. Once upon a time conceit entered the heart of the Divine Sage Nârada, and he thought that there was no greater devotee than himself. Reading his heart, the Lord Srì Vishnu said, "Nârada, go to such and such a place, there is a great Bhakta of mine there, and cultivate his acquaintance." Nârada went there and found an agriculturist, who rose early in the morning, pronounced the name of Hari only once, and taking his plough went out to till the ground all day long. At night he went to bed after pronouncing the name of Hari once more. Nârada said within himself, "How can this rustic be called a lover of God? I see him busily engaged in worldly duties, and he has no signs of a pious man in him." Nârada then went back to the Lord and said all that he thought of his new acquaintance. The Lord said, "Nârada, take this cup full of oil, go round this city and come back with it, but beware lest a drop of it fall to the ground." Nârada did as he was told, and on his return

Sri Ramakrishna.

he was asked, "Well, Nârada, how often did you remember me in your walk?" "Not once, my Lord," replied Nârada, "and how could I when I had to watch this cup brimming over with oil?" The Lord then said, "This one cup of oil did so divert your attention that even you did forget me altogether, but look to that rustic who, carrying the heavy load of a family, still remembers me twice every day."

551. A tame mungoose had its home high up on the wall of a house. One end of a rope was tied to its neck, while the other end was fastened to a weight. The mungoose with the appendage runs and plays in the parlor or in the yard of the house, but no sooner does it get frightened than it at once runs up and hides itself in its home on the wall. But it cannot stay there long, as the weight at the other end of the rope draws it down, and it is constrained to leave its home. Similarly, a man has his home high up at the feet of the Almighty. Whenever he is frightened by adversity and misfortune he goes up to his God, his true home; but in a short time he is constrained to come

down into the world by its irresistible attractions.

552. A rich man puts his Sircar (a superintending clerk) in charge of his garden. When visitors look in, the Sircar is all attention to them. He takes them through the different parts of the garden and the house attached to it, saying, ·'These, gentlemen, are our mango trees. These are our *lichi golapjam*, etc. Here, you see, is our drawing-room. Over there are our oil paintings and other pictures, so splendid, etc.

Now suppose the Sircar is caught by his master fishing against his order in the garden lake. Do you know how he is dealt with? Why, he is ordered peremptorily to leave the garden. And it was, bear in mind, the very same man who was so warmly talking of "*our* this" and "*our* that."

· The "mine" or "our" of the Sircar comes of ajnan (ignorance of truth).

553. The calf bellows "Hamma" or "Aham" (I). Now look at the troubles

Sri Ramakrishna.

caused by this, its Ahamkâra, which says "I," "I." In the first place, when grown up it is yoked to the plough. It works from dawn to eve alike in sun and rain. It may be killed by the butcher. Its flesh is eaten. Its skin is tanned into hide and made into shoes. Drums are also made with it, which are mercilessly beaten sometimes with the hand and at others with the drumstick. It is only when out of its entrails are made strings for the bows used for carding cotton that the troubles of the poor creature are over. And that is because it no longer says "Hamma (I), Hamma (I)," but "Tuhum, Tuhum (It is Thou, it is Thou)."

The moral is that Mukti (freedom) is within the reach of him alone who has learnt the lesson of complete self-abnegation, perfect forgetfulness of self.

It also teaches that unless the vital parts (entrails of the calf) are struck, Aham (I-ness) can hardly be got rid of. One scarcely says "Tuhum" (Thou) until one is cut to the quick, that is, loses riches, sons, and the like. Even when struck by such severe blows, the "Thou-ness" may or may not come to replace the "I-ness."

The Sayings of

554. Greed brings woe, while content-
ment is all happiness. A barber was once
passing under a haunted tree when he
heard a voice say, "Wilt thou accept of
seven jars of gold?" The barber looked
round, but could see no one. The mys-
terious voice again repeated the words,
and the cupidity of the barber being
greatly roused by the spontaneous offer
of such wealth, he spoke aloud, "When
the merciful God is so good as to take pity
even on a poor barber like me, is there
anything to be said as to my accepting
the kind offer so generously made?" At
once the reply came, "Go home, I have
already carried the jars thither." The
barber ran in hot haste to his house and
was transported to see the promised jars
there. He opened them one after another
and saw them all filled, save one which was
half filled. Now arose in the heart of the
barber the desire of filling this last jar.
So he sold all his gold and silver ornaments
and converted them into coins and threw
them into the jar. But the jar still remained empty. He now began to starve
himself and his family by living upon in-
sufficient, coarse, and cheap food, throw

224

Sri Ramakrishna.

ing all his savings into the jar, but the jar remained as empty as ever. The barber then requested the King to increase his pay as it was not sufficient to maintain him and his family. As he was a favorite of the King, the latter granted his request. The barber now began to save all his pay and emoluments and throw them all into the jar, but the greedy jar showed no sign of being filled. He now began to live by begging, and became as wretched and miserable as possible. One day the King, seeing his sad plight, inquired of him by saying, "Hallo! when thy pay was half of what thou gettest now, thou wast far happier and more cheerful, contented, and healthy; but with double that pay I see thee morose, careworn, and dejected. Now what is the matter with thee? Hast thou accepted the seven jars of gold?" The barber was taken aback by this home-thrust, and with clasped hands asked the King as to who had informed his majesty about the matter. The King answered, "Whosoever accepts the riches of a Yaksha is sure to be reduced to such an abject and wretched plight. I have known thee through this invariable sign. Do away with the money at once. Thou canst not spend a farthing of it. That money is for hoarding and not for spending." The barber was brought to his senses by this advice and went to the haunted tree and said, "O Yaksha, take back thy gold," and he returned home to find the seven jars vanished, taking with them his life-long savings. Nevertheless he began to live happily thereafter.

INDEX.

I.

MARGINAL HEADINGS.

Index.

Index.

Index.

Index.

Index.

II.

PARABLES.

Index.

Index.

COSIMO is a specialty publisher of books and publications that inspire, inform, and engage readers. Our mission is to offer unique books to niche audiences around the world.

COSIMO BOOKS publishes books and publications for innovative authors, nonprofit organizations, and businesses. **COSIMO BOOKS** specializes in bringing books back into print, publishing new books quickly and effectively, and making these publications available to readers around the world.

COSIMO CLASSICS offers a collection of distinctive titles by the great authors and thinkers throughout the ages. At **COSIMO CLASSICS** timeless works find new life as affordable books, covering a variety of subjects including: Business, Economics, History, Personal Development, Philosophy, Religion & Spirituality, and much more!

COSIMO REPORTS publishes public reports that affect your world, from global trends to the economy, and from health to geopolitics.

CPSIA information can be obtained
at www.ICGtesting.com
Printed in the USA
BVHW071945291221
625096BV00001B/48